Hideo Okamoto

Exchange Prisoner and War Plan Orange

CLAUDE MORITA

Japanese Cultural Center of Hawaiʻi
Honolulu, Hawaiʻi

Printed in the United States of America

24 23 22 21 20 19 1 2 3 4 5 6

Library of Congress Cataloging-in-Publication Data

Names: Morita, Claude, author.
Title: Hideo Okamoto : exchange prisoner and War Plan Orange / Claude Morita.
Description: Honolulu, Hawaii : Japanese Cultural Center of Hawaii, [2019]
Identifiers: LCCN 2019000162 | ISBN 9780824881689 (pbk. ; alk. paper)
Subjects: LCSH: Okamoto, Hideo, 1892–1979. | Japanese Americans—Evacuation and relocation, 1942–1945. | World War, 1939–1945—Evacuation of civilians—United States. | World War, 1939–1945—Japan—Forced repatriation.
Classification: LCC D769.8.A6 M67 2019 | DDC 940.53089956073—dc23
LC record available at https://lccn.loc.gov/2019000162

This publication is printed on acid-free paper
and meets the guidelines for permanence and durability
of the Council of Library Resources.

Cover photo: Hideo's American born niece Sochiko,
nephew Richard, and daughter Joy at the Ashbury Park Broadwalk,
New Jersey, in the 1930's. Courtesy of Joy Tsuzuki.

Printer-ready files provided by the author.

Distributed by
University of Hawai'i Press
2840 Kolowalu Street
Honolulu, Hawai'i 96822
www.uhpress.hawaii.edu

Contents

Foreword

Dennis M. Ogawa

Author Jan Jarboe Russell writes in her book *The Train to Crystal City: FDR's Secret Prisoner Exchange Program and America's Only Family Internment Camp During World War II,* that on May 5, 2015:

> Late in the afternoon, I walked into the East Room of the White House to attend President Barack Obama's annual Cinco de Mayo celebration, which recognizes the contributions of millions of Americans of Latino descent. At the end of Obama's remarks, he pressed Congress to pass immigration reform and cited the following passage from a speech that Franklin Roosevelt made in 1938: "Remember, remember always that all of us, and you and I especially, are descended from immigrants and revolutionaries." The room exploded with applause, but the reference seemed deeply ironic to me as I reflected on the memories of the children of the Crystal City Internment Camp. Four years after Roosevelt spoke those words, thousands of immigrant fathers and mothers and their American-born children were interned in the camp at the southern tip of Texas.

With due respect to Jan Jarboe Russell or President Barack Obama, no matter what the occasion, the author of this book, Claude Morita only thinks of one word when it comes to a reference of FDR: racist. Years before 1938, FDR focused on planning a war against Japan. He saw nothing different between people living on the Japanese archipelago and American citizens of Japanese descent. Nor did he oppose or countermand his generals, including John L. DeWitt, who advocated that a "Jap is a Jap." On February 19, 1942, FDR signed Executive Order 9066 which imprisoned 120,000 persons of Japanese ancestry, two-thirds of them Americans, in concentration camps. Morita's family was among those incarcerated.

But even before Pearl Harbor and the barbwire camps, Morita experienced FDR's racial harshness. He writes:

> I personally encountered President Franklin Delano Roosevelt's animosity on 28 September, 1937 in what can only be interpreted as racist hate. I will likely never forget the occasion for its less than auspicious celebration. The event was focused on his dedication of Timberline Lodge on snow covered Mt. Hood, a beautiful reminder of the Northwest in Hood River, Oregon. FDR arrived in Hood River Valley for the event after inspecting nearby Bonneville Dam on the Columbia River which was still under construction.
>
> The trip was to remind his constituency of his accomplishments in improving the economic conditions in the Northwest, still in the grips of depression. Valley residents lined the route of his motorcade to Timberline Lodge through the valley along the Loop Highway that runs the length of the valley. The student body of Odell Grade School, perhaps 200 students and teachers, was let out of school to greet him on the highway leading to Timberline Lodge. Other residents of Odell joined us at the Y intersection connecting the Loop to the town of Odell. We carried no banners, signs, or flags. It was an exciting event of good feeling and optimism.
>
> We stood no more than six feet from the slowly passing caravan of cars which, in those days, had no protective security or police escort. FDR's sedan was open, a convertible in the sense it could be enclosed if necessary. My third grade classmates and I shouted, "President Roosevelt! Welcome to Hood River!" It was an occasion for much cheering and smiling.
>
> When I made eye contact, his expression froze and changed. He gave me a hard, dirty look. It was clear and unmistakable. It was hate expressed in a public celebration. Hawaiians would describe FDR as giving me the "stink eye." If looks could kill, I was a dead pigeon. Eye contact is normally an important sign of confidence, respect, social communication, and healing which are often publicly acknowledged.

> In this case, however, it was an unmistakable "dirty look" at close range by an adult at a child. Perhaps it was my big ears, my squinty epicanthic fold, or slightly different skin color that attracted his attention. At any rate, amidst the shouting and cheering, FDR looked directly at me and glared. It was shocking. I did not expect such behavior from a President. I walked back to school in stunned silence with my happy, excited classmates.

Claude Morita recognizes the racism, the injustice, and oppressions heaped upon individuals, families, and children of Japanese descent living in America. Government agencies, military establishments, and elected officials at the highest levels were culprits involved with America's war against Japan. Morita uncovers many unconstitutional actions directed at the Japanese. He tells us about declassified documents filed at the National Archives in Washington DC. Of particular note are materials tied to War Plan Orange, which shows that America had been preparing for war against Japan since 1898, not December 7, 1941.

To personalize the consequences of War Plan Orange and the unlawful events it precipitated, Morita shares with us the life story of Hideo Okamoto, an Issei—first generation immigrant Japanese—who was jailed and transferred to a concentration camp as an enemy spy. Based on fabricated charges made up by the Office of Naval Intelligence, he was used as an exchange prisoner of war by FDR.

Immediately on December 7, 1941, Okamoto was arrested by the FBI and jailed for almost half a year, first in Florida, then in Tennessee and Virginia. On June 18, 1942, he was placed aboard the neutral exchange ship *Gripsholm*, a Swedish liner that sailed from Ellis Island, New York. He would be part of the first exchange of prisoners of war with Japan. Morita says, "The ship even had Nisei children, little American children aboard... railroaded because there were no real honest to goodness prisoners of war in the U.S. to exchange. Instead, the criterion for a prisoner of war was simply looking Japanese." Hideo Okamoto was delivered, traded as a prisoner of war, and forced to live out his life in Japan. He was abandoned and forgotten by America.

In recounting Okamoto's story, Morita provides us with many insights of how individuals lived their lives and survived World War II. He calls to our attention Okamoto's outlook and way of conduct. Morita cannot help but be amazed that throughout Okamoto's ordeal, he never got angry. Most people will say that anger at racism is wholly justified—nothing can be more insidious than the venom of racial prejudice. But why then was anger not expressed? Much of the studies on Japanese Americans, especially the Issei, refer to the Japanese values of *shikata ga nai*—it cannot be helped—or *gaman*—to endure the unbearable with dignity and forbearance.

For Morita, the answer differs. His thinking is based on personally asking Japanese in Japan and Japanese scholars why Issei rarely got angry. The answer Morita received was "surprising and nearly unanimously expressed." It was all about *Kanyo*, a characteristic of the Japanese personality associated with Buddhist teachings that looks upon people with tolerance and leniency. This conduct forms around spiritual generosity. *Kanyo* is a basic characteristic of Japanese, "but is rarely talked about. It is for Japanese to do so."

Soon after his arrival in Japan, Okamoto found work in a metal factory owned by Mitsubishi Company because he was bilingual and the factory was using Americans captured when war broke out. Okamoto was the liaison. This was not an easy job because of the Japanese military's severe discipline, security, and the lack of food. Okamoto's character allowed for some sense of humaneness.

In his account of Okamoto and *Kanyo*, Morita makes us realize the value of a humanistic approach with the past. This is reflective, particularly in his telling and moving stories of how Okamoto cared for the American soldiers. They were so young, mostly under twenty. He wanted to make their life less miserable. This was tantamount to treason, but he had to try.

After the war ended on August 15th, 1945, the International War Crimes Tribunals were held. Japanese military officers and others were identified and punished for any mistreatment of the American prisoners of war. Okamoto was never put on trial. The American prisoners all signed a petition on his behalf.

Claude Morita gives us a dramatic lesson of American history. The U.S. war against Japan was a crime and though people of Japanese ancestry living in America, even their American born children, were the victims of that crime, they sought to not lose their spirit and sense of humanity.

Morita's book is one to read and reread for generations to come.

Acknowledgments

Thank you to Alfred and Mattie Dethman for teaching me about true democracy in America. He said, "Don't go to the camp. I'll hide you in the mountains." Senior Superintendent Toshihiro Shirasawa, for tutoring me on Japanese investigating work. To the Naval Criminal Investigative Service (Far East Division) for giving me the challenge of distinguishing the character of evil in society. To the Vietnamese people, for teaching me understanding, forgiveness, and hope for the world.

Preface

I have worked decades in the US military history programs at Pacific Air Force and Seventh Air Force in Vietnam. I have also been an intelligence operations specialist with Naval Criminal Investigative Service in Yokosuka and Sasebo Naval Bases in Japan. NCIS work requires the test of courts. My recent research of documents declassified in 1991 was in the National Archives in Washington DC. I also maintained the services of Nichimy Corporation in Tokyo to research in the National Archives. The declassified documents show that the US planned the war against Japan in about 1898. This book, War Plan Orange, will rattle a lot of international cages.

With this in mind, I want to also say that I worked for the 6004th Air Intelligence Service Squadron in Japan and Korea in the Occupation of Japan and the War in Korea. My co-worker was Joy Okamoto, whose father, Hideo Okamoto, is mentioned a great deal in this book. Because of War Plan Orange, he was unconstitutionally exchanged as a so-called prisoner of war, along with other Issei and their children. Some of those children, many from Hawaii and the West Coast, are still alive and remain abandoned in Japan. They must not be forgotten.

Introduction

Known for his courage and public speaking, Henry David Thoreau argued that individuals should not permit governments to overrule or atrophy their consciences and thereby be made into agents of injustice. Thoreau was motivated in part by his disgust with slavery in America, the emotionalism behind US motives in the one-sided Mexican-American War (1846–1848), the madness of the California Gold Rush (1848–1855), and the racism endemic in his time. He clearly discerned the undemocratic, hegemonic impulses of the US government which have remained into the 21st century.

Thoreau's wisdom applies to governments and citizens, in general, at any time, but especially when a war is involved. The US government developed War Plan Orange, an offensive strategy against Japan, in strict secrecy for more than 90 years, from about 1898 until 1991. The secrecy was necessary because the plans revealed motives that violated many of the idealized themes of the US Constitution and involved citizens in unjust actions, just as Thoreau warned.

War Plan Orange shows that the Pacific War between the United States and Japan did not begin on 7 December, 1941. Rather, the US started the war against Japan in 1898. Under modern standards for classifying government documents, War Plan Orange would have been classified Top Secret, as its revelation would have caused exceptionally grave damage to the national security of the United States. War Plan Orange refers to a series of United States Joint Army and Navy Board war plans for managing hostilities against Japan between 1898–1941, or until provocations by the US could no longer be endured by Japan.

Japan's interests and territories in the Pacific Ocean following

World War I were a matter of concern to US military planners who sought to counter or divest Japan of economically significant locations. Japan has few natural resources, and the shortage of raw materials during industrialization in the Meiji Period (1868–1912) meant that the development of the Japanese colonial empire was a political and economic necessity. By the outbreak of World War I, the empire included Taiwan, Korea, the Ryukyu Islands, the southern half of Sakhalin Island, the Kurile Islands, and Port Arthur (Dalian). The policy of *Nanshin-ron* or "Southern Expansion Doctrine," popular with the Imperial Japanese Navy, held that Southeast Asia and the Pacific Islands were the area of greatest potential value to the Japanese Empire for economic and territorial expansion.

The Anglo-Japanese Alliance of 1902 had been signed primarily to serve the common interests of Japan and the US for opposing Russian expansion. Among the other provisions, the treaty called on each party to support the other in a war against more than one power, although it did not require a signatory state to go to war to aid the other. Within hours of Britain's declaration of war on Germany in 1914, Japan invoked the treaty and offered to declare war on the German Empire if it could take German territories in China and the South Pacific. The British government officially asked Japan for assistance in destroying the raiders from the Imperial German Navy in and around Chinese waters, and Japan sent Germany an ultimatum demanding that it vacate China and the Marshall, Mariana, and Caroline islands. The ultimatum went unanswered and Japan formally declared war on Germany on 23 August 1914.

Japan participated in a joint operation with British forces in autumn 1914 in the Siege of Tsingtao (Qingdao) to capture the Kiautschou Bay concession in China's Shandong Province. The Japanese Navy was tasked with pursuing and destroying the German East Asiatic Squadron and the protection of the shipping lanes for Allied commerce in the Pacific and Indian Oceans. During this operation, the Japanese Navy seized the German possessions in the Marianas, Carolines, Marshall Islands and Palau groups by October 1914. Japan's actions, though based on the UK-Japan alliance, were negatively viewed by the US. The details for War Plan Orange became more refined.

War Plan Orange's goal was hostilities, meticulously planned by every agency in all military units down to small boat operators and radio communication sites. Although War Plan Orange originated in the 1890s, the plan's status by 1922 is explained to show how thorough-going hostilities with Japan were in the minds of US leaders. To take this into account, I enclose the following outline of studies that have been made in the War Plans Division during the years 1920–22. These studies, summarized by Major John J. King, are numbered serially.

1. Dated December 29, 1920, was prepared with a view to determining priority in the preparation of war plans and to establishing sound basis for developing War Plan Orange. Copies of this memorandum were furnished to the other divisions of the General Staff and to the Naval members of the Planning Committee for their comments and suggestions. The comments and suggestions received are attached to Number 2.

2. This is a memorandum of January 15, 1921, for General William George Haan, the Director of War Plans Division, enclosing the comments referred to above. Attached to this memorandum, and numbered 2-E, is a revised draft, dated January 15, 1921, of the memorandum for the Chief of Staff about the basis for the development of war plans.

3. Dated January 19, 1921, is a memorandum by the Director of the War Plans Division stating that the Chief of Staff had approved giving priority to the Orange War Plan and desired that a basic plan be prepared and submitted to him. This memorandum also outlines the form that the basic plan should take.

4. Dated January 20, 1921, is a memorandum for the Chief of Staff with the subject: A Basis for the Development of War Plans. It recommends that the Orange Plan be given priority and recommends certain principles upon which the plan should be based.

5. In a memorandum of January 28, 1921, the Director of the War Plans Division submitted to the other divisions of the General Staff a preliminary draft of War Plan Orange with request for their comments and recommendations.

6. Consists of an unsigned memorandum for the Chief of Staff of the War Plans Division from January 20, 1921 regarding A Basis for the Development of War Plans, a copy of a preliminary draft of War Plan Orange, and comments by the Director of Operations, the Direc-

tor of Military Intelligence, the Director of the Supply Division, and the Naval members of the Joint Army and Navy Planning Committee. General Haan did not sign the memorandum, and returned it with a memorandum from August 8, 1921 asking for additional information on the number of troops required, the rate at which they would be sent across the Pacific, and the amount of time it would take to establish lines of communication.

7. Dated 3 December, 1921, is a memorandum for the Chief of War Plan Orange, which consists of (a) An estimate of the situation, (b) Decision, (c) Mission of the Blue Navy, (d) Mission of the Blue Army; (e) Conclusions, and (f) Procedure that should be followed in the further development of the Orange Plan. Attached to this memorandum is an unsigned estimate dated March 27, 1922, prepared by the Naval members of the Planning Committee and setting forth their opinion as to the number of troops that the Army should furnish for the various stages of the advance across the Pacific up to and including the landing of 300,000 men on the China coast. The original of the above-mentioned memorandum of December 3, 1921 was transmitted December 16, 1921, to the Naval members.

The survival of the United States government was not at stake in 1898 nor in the 1920's. Its population was not at risk either. But U.S. military planners behaved secretly as if dangers existed.

No member of the planning staff opposed any part of the plans war with Japan; they all rose in rank thereafter. The likelihood of opposition to War Plan Orange was miniscule with General of the Army John J. Pershing approving on 7 July, 1923. The scope and extent of the war against Japan was overwhelming. At no time was there any opposition to the war against Japan. Its racist orientation was clear from a number of perspectives, including officers who publicly voiced their antipathy; one of the more hostile was General John L. DeWitt's persistent diatribe, "A Jap is a Jap is a Jap." President Franklin Delano Roosevelt did not oppose or countermand his subordinates. In the making of War Plan Orange, with such individuals as DeWitt driving policy, it is not surprising that deplorable actions would occur against those of Japanese ancestry.

Soon after Japan's 7 December, 1941 attack on Pearl Harbor, Hawaii, all ethnic Japanese Americans—US citizens as well as legal residents—living on the West Coast of America, including Alaska, were ordered into concentration camps the government prepared for them. Some Eskimos and Inuits were misidentified as Japanese and incarcerated. The removal and imprisonment began on March 23, 1942, with the resettlement of citizens living in Los Angeles. On that date, General DeWitt issued new orders applying to Japanese-Americans, setting an 8 p.m. to 6 a.m. curfew and banning ownership of firearms, radios, cameras, and other contraband. DeWitt stated, "Let me warn the affected aliens and citizens the proclamation provisions will bring immediate punishment." This application of military law was made without a single instance of subversive activity.

Northern California followed in April, as DeWitt declared, "We plan to increase the tempo of the evacuation as fast as possible." Citizens in specific areas were required to report to their designated "Civil Control Station," where they would then be taken to an Assembly Center for relocation. All told, DeWitt ordered the removal and internment of 110,000 men, women and children of Japanese ancestry from their homes to internment camps. Federal judge James Alger Fee, of Portland, Oregon, ruled in November 1943 that American citizens could not be detained without a proclamation of martial law. DeWitt's response was that "All military orders and proclamations of this headquarters remain in full force and effect."

After the "relocation" of Japanese Americans was complete, DeWitt lifted curfew restrictions on Italian Americans on October 19 and on German Americans on December 24, 1942. Technically, the curfew was "inapplicable to the Japanese since all members of this group were removed from the affected zones." DeWitt was opposed to War Relocation Authority efforts to distinguish loyal from disloyal Japanese Americans and to the creation of an all-Japanese combat unit. He testified before Congress, in 1943, that he would "use every proper means" at his disposal to stop the resettlement of Japanese Americans outside camp and their eventual return to the West Coast after the war. His Final Report also explained his position that their race made it impossible to determine their loyalty. Sadly, individuals of Japanese ancestry living in America such as Hideo Okamoto would be deeply affected by War Plan Orange and by the actions of people such as De Witt who helped conceive it.

CHAPTER 1

Hope and Aspirations

Born on October 25, 1892, Hideo Okamoto began life in Yokohama, Japan, maintaining family traditions of honor in life that centered on Japan's warrior class. Hideo had ties to one of the four predominant samurai clans—the Minamoto, Tachibana, Taira, and Fujiwara—that survived and persevered through the 19th Century. His was a life of virtue and discipline in a rapidly changing world into which Japan found, on the one hand glory and, on the other, dismal betrayal. Hideo expected life to be lived honorably and considered compassion to be of the utmost importance. He was going to try to live by these qualities anywhere he went in the world. And it was in Japan and the United States where he was to spend his life, but it was full of surprises.

Seeking opportunities for the family and himself, Hideo's father, Minekichi, was an adventurous Japanese and left for America. Of his four sons, Hideo and Shunzo travelled to America while his brothers Shoji and Hiroyuki remained in Japan. One sister, Fuku, also remained in Japan and the other, Fuji, married a member of the Kaneko family and moved to France to expand the family's ties. In his youth in Yokohama, Hideo immersed himself in study, field trips to notable sites in and near the city, after school tutoring, and a home life favoring male privileges in a samurai family. He and his classmates would visit statues of Kinjiro Ninomiya, located at many places in Japan. The statues are unique. A young man is shown with a load of firewood on his back. But he is also reading a book; he is studying while working. There is no time to waste. Nearly every prefecture in Japan has such a statue. With such emphasis on self-betterment, students are inspired to follow suit.

With his father and a brother already in the United States,

Hideo knew that he would be embarking on a life of adventure overseas. He looked for patterns and models to follow. An especially compelling figure was Daimyo (大名) Masamune Date who, in the years 1613 through 1620, established relations with the Pope in Rome and founded a Japanese community in Spain. He had hoped that he would secure the consent of Spain to participate in lucrative trade in the continent between the two oceans. Going elsewhere for expanding visions was Hideo's mission as well.

Hideo learned the fundamentals of being a Japanese in a changing world in his most formative years. At about ten years of age, Hideo Okamoto traveled alone aboard a ship bound for San Francisco in the United States from Yokohama in 1903 to join his father and older brother. The new country was full of opportunities unheard of in Japan. A person could establish any business he wished, move to any region in the expansive country, speak freely about any subject at any location. His father instructed Hideo to join the Okamoto family in America. Details are not available about his life on the ship that transported him, except that he enjoyed the trip and his freedom despite the danger of being washed overboard during storms.

Undoubtedly, Hideo was excited about moving to America, which had only established relations with Japan a mere fifty years earlier. Hideo never disclosed stories of his youth in Japan to his daughter, Yoshiko Joy. But she gained some insight from Hideo's mother. Having raised him for ten years, his mother readily distinguished between Hideo and his older brother Shunzo. She said, "My younger son was quick and responsive. But the older son was vacillating, hesitant to a fault." She was not critical of either, but, as a mother, cared a great deal about her family. Hideo's quickness actions could be risky, however. His daughter said, "I remember him telling me about a wagon that he had made himself. He hitched this wagon to a streetcar and would sit in it and get rides up and down hills in San Francisco. I'm sure that it was against the rules." She continued, "I know very little of him as a youth in San Francisco. He was good baseball player, the team catcher. I believe in his youth, he and George Togasaki (later president of the newspaper *Japan Times*) played on the same team."

Hideo attended high school in San Francisco, which was a segregated school where only Japanese attended. Hideo learned that discriminatory rules applied to people in America who were not white. It was disconcerting, but he did not publicly complain about what was obviously a wrong. With the Okamoto family emphasis on education and purpose in life, he then attended a junior college and graduated with a major in business. Hideo intended to become a businessman in America. Because of the reality of US-Japan relations, and the subsequent implementation of War Plan Orange, things in his life did not play out as he expected.

War Plan Orange was created by the Office of Naval Intelligence in the late 1890s and remained active into the 1940s. Among its authors were Theodore Roosevelt and Franklin Delano Roosevelt during their respective terms as Assistant Secretary of the Navy. When needed, operational orders implemented actual military operations against Japan. Such operations were kept from the American public to convey the impression that the aggressor was Japan. Conventional wisdom is that Japan initiated war in 1941. Nothing could be further from the truth; the top secret document" Joint Army-Navy Board No. 355," which authorized American bombing raids against Japan, is signed by the Secretaries of War and Navy, and bears Franklin Roosevelt's initials and a handwritten date, July 23, 1941—more than four months before the Japanese attack against Pearl Harbor.

As finally laid out in "Joint Army-Navy Board No. 355," an air strike force of 500 Lockheed Hudson bombers was to be organized as "The Second American Volunteer Group." Its mission would be the pre-emptive bombing of Japan. The strategic objective of JB 355 was the "destruction of Japanese factories . . . to cripple munitions and essential articles for maintenance of economic structure in Japan." From bases about 1,300 miles away in eastern China, the American bombers would strike Japan's industrial centers, including Osaka, Nagasaki, Yokohama and Tokyo. These air strikes would have unavoidably claimed the lives of many civilians. By contrast, the Japanese planes that attacked Pearl Harbor carefully avoided civilian targets.

Theodore Roosevelt and Franklin Delano Roosevelt, during their terms as Assistant Secretary of the Navy, contributed details of War Plan Orange for attaining goals with the use of force. Neither President Herbert Hoover nor General Douglas MacArthur agreed with the aims of the war planning nor the eventual, fateful use of atomic bombs. For war against Japan, War Plan Orange consisted of three phases. Phase I: The U.S. expected the loss of the lightly defended outposts south and west of Japan. The US knew it could not defend these outposts successfully. Orange envisioned the concentration of US Navy ships at their homeports. These forces could be deployed from the Eastern Pacific on short notice. Phase II: The US, with superior naval and air power, would advance west. Through small-scale attacks against Japanese occupied islands they would capture them and establish supply routes and overseas bases. Because of U.S. production power, planners anticipated that the Philippine Islands would be reoccupied within two to three years. Phase III: The U.S. would then advance toward Japan utilizing islands that were parallel to and near Asia. These newly acquired bases could choke Japanese trade and allow air bombardment of Japanese cities and industry, leading to victory without invasion of the Japanese homeland.

The scenario for countering Japan had existed since the turn of the century when the United States, after its war with Spain, found itself in possession of many islands in the Pacific Ocean, notably the Philippines and Guam, which it could neither administer nor adequately defend. The military aspects of the situation called for close cooperation between the Army and Navy and in 1903 led to creation of the joint Army-Navy Board, usually known as the Joint Board.

From its beginning, the board concerned itself with prospects of war with Japan, particularly after Japan emerged victorious from the Russo-Japanese war in 1904–05. A fundamental assumption by the board was that the Philippines would always be Japan's first wartime objective.The Army-Navy Board developed the first war strategy in 1904–05. The usual pattern was for the joint plan to be augmented by individual service plans which were constantly reviewed and refined each year depending on military necessity, the moods of Congress, and the international situation. As War Plan Orange grew in complexity, the service plans themselves were augmented by other plans, such as those created by Naval Communications and Naval Intelligence.

The strategy for war in the Pacific with Japan was the only part of American military planning that had a long, continuous history. Since the early 1900's, it had been evident that the United States government, if it should ever oppose Japanese imperial aims without the support of Great Britain and Russia, might have to choose between withdrawal from the Far East or war with Japan. As previously mentioned, the events of World War I, a war centered in Europe, however, put a serious dent into War Plan Orange. Japan was drawn into the conflict when the British government requested assistance on August 14, 1914. Japan formally declared war against Germany on August 23, 1914 and with Austria-Hungary on August 25, 1914. With the American entry into World War I on April 6, 1917, the United States and Japan found themselves on the same side, despite their increasingly bad relations over China and battle for influence in the Pacific. US war planners must have been dismayed.

Acting in its own interests while assisting Britain, Japanese forces quickly occupied German-leased territories in the Far East. On September 2, 1914, Japanese landed on China's Shantung province and surrounded the German settlement at Qingdao. During October, acting nearly independent of the civil government, the Imperial Navy seized several of Germany's island colonies in the Pacific—the Mariana, Caroline, and Marshall Islands—finding virtually no resistance.

On December 18, 1916, the British Admiralty again requested naval assistance from Japan. Two cruisers were sent to Cape Town, South Africa, and four destroyers were sent to the Mediterranean for basing out of Malta. Rear-Admiral Kozo Sato on the cruiser *Akashi* and 10th and 11th destroyer units (eight destroyers) arrived in Malta on April 13, 1917. Eventually this Second Special Squadron consisted of three cruisers, 14 destroyers, two sloops, and one tender. It was a formidable force. The squadron carried out escort duties for troop transports and anti-submarine operations. No ship was lost, but on June 11, 1917 a Kaba-class destroyer was hit by a torpedo from an Austro-Hungarian submarine off Crete; 59 Japanese sailors died. The Japanese squadron made a total of 348 escort sorties from Malta, escorting 788 ships carrying around 700,000 soldiers, contributing greatly to the war effort.

In return for this assistance, Great Britain recognized Japan's territorial gains in Shantung and in the Pacific islands north of the equator. War Plan Orange became overtaken by events. Threats to the United States had assumptions of rising Japanese imperialism, the exhaustion of Russia and its alienation from the Western world, the disarmament of the United States, and the withdrawal of the United States from its close relations with the European colonial powers. In the Pacific, the Japanese had strengthened its position by taking the Mariana, Caroline, and Marshall Islands. The League of Nations confirmed Japanese control of these islands in 1920 by a mandate.

After the 1922 Washington Naval Treaty, the United States began to fall behind Japan in the construction of new naval vessels. In the early 1920s, the United States was faced with the unpleasant prospect not only of the continuation of a prewar Anglo-Japanese alliance with unfavorable balance of power implications; but with a superior Japanese fleet in the Pacific, occupying the former German islands which could cut US lines of communication to Australia and the Philippines. This made the US defense of its Philippine possession difficult if not impossible.

For long periods in its history, the Philippines suffered under the colonial rule of outsiders, including the US. Spain gave up the Philippines to the United States after the US victory in the Spanish-American War. During the war, Philippine revolutionaries declared independence for the islands and the establishment of the First Philippine Republic. The United States, however, would not recognize the budding First Philippine Republic after Spain ceded the islands in 1898; the Philippine-American War broke out. The First Republic was defeated and the archipelago was administered under an Insular Government. The war resulted in the deaths of tens of thousands of combatants as well as a hundred thousand civilians, mostly from a cholera epidemic.

The Philippine Organic Act of 1902 provided for the establishment of a bicameral legislature composed of an upper house consisting of the Philippine Commission, an appointed body with both American and Filipino members, and a popularly elected lower house, the Philippine Assembly. The Philippines became a U.S. colony. It was patterned after European imperialism, with benevolent colonial practices. English joined Spanish as an official language; English language education was made compulsory. In 1916, the United States passed the Philippine Autonomy Act and committed itself to granting independence to the Philippines "as soon as a stable government can be established therein." As a step to full independence in 1946, partial autonomy as a Commonwealth was granted in 1935.

Self-determination was challenged at different locations worldwide. The exercise of the power of one nation over the other, its immorality, is continually challenged by reasonable thinkers of the world. At the Washington Conference in 1921, the US succeeded in replacing the Anglo-Japanese alliance with a four-power treaty with Britain, France, and Japan. This treaty limited US and UK base-building in the Pacific in return for reluctant Japanese acceptance of apparently unfavorable ratios in naval strength.

Although not at first seen as a good treaty for Japan, several factors came to make it so. Among these were an old-fashioned British dreadnought fleet which effectively eliminated the British Asiatic Fleet as a force; a moratorium on battleship construction which had the United States scrap 28 vessels including eleven capital ships in various stages of completion; a US commitment to a two-ocean navy which meant that not all new ships joined the Pacific Fleet; and the base-building restrictions of the four-power treaty. Collectively, these measures left Japan in a position of local superiority and in a dominant position regarding the coast and approaches to China.

In the early 1920s, the war plans divisions of the War Department and the Navy Department drew up contingency plans for what they saw to be a two-theater world war fought in the Atlantic and the Pacific. In Plan Orange, US strategists theorized that there would be a war with Japan over resources and territory in the Pacific. This was the very antithesis of maintaining peace that democracies are obliged to nurture and propagate. Hostile action and plans are the characteristics of aggressors.

In War Plan Red, the Atlantic Strategic War Plan, strategists theorized that there would be a war with Great Britain. They did this because England was locked in a strategic alliance with Japan, the Anglo-Japanese Alliance of 1902, which was renewed and lasted until the Washington Conference of 1921–22. American planners thought that England's imperial reach would bring it into conflict with the US.

Another contingency war plan they developed was the Red-Orange Plan, which hypothesized a two-theater war, seeking to win first in the Atlantic, against England, while fighting a holding battle in the Pacific, and then defeating Japan. When World War II broke out, US planners simply dusted off the old Red-Orange Plan and substituted Germany for England in the Atlantic Theater. The broader strategy and the resources to carry it out, including defense construction and mobilization of reserves, was essentially the same. The main point to be learned here is that a theoretical planning construct reflects the real thinking of top leadership of the US. It does not make an enemy of a country; it presumes such is the fact. The unfortunate fact of race distinctions in American history and societal behavior plague conduct at all levels.

England made a strategic policy choice at the Washington Conference, deciding to cast its lot with the United States, and turned out to be a close ally by the late-1930s. But the Red-Orange Plan stayed on the US Joint Army-Navy Board's agenda through 1939. The first, post-World War I plan for war in the Pacific, developed between 1921 and 1924 reviewed America's unfavorable strategic position and reaffirmed Japan as the enemy. World War I was Japan's entry onto the world stage as a very significant player and the US could not counter her influence. Consequently, War Plan Orange became temporarily irrelevant. War motivations with a definite racist tinge were stopped, but as an event to be revived.

An Orange driven war with Japan would be primarily a naval war fought in the Pacific. So far as anyone could foresee, there would be no requirement for large ground armies. There was a possibility, of course, that Japan would attack the Panama Canal, Hawaii, and even the West Coast, but no real danger of Japan seizing and occupying any of these places. The strategic concept adopted by the planners in the event of hostilities was to fight "an offensive war, primarily naval . . . with the objective of establishing at the earliest date American sea power in the western Pacific in strength superior to that of Japan."

To do this, the United States would require a base in the Pacific capable of serving the entire U.S. Fleet. Since the only base west of Pearl Harbor large enough for this purpose was in Manila Bay, it would be essential, the planners said, to hold the bay in case of war and be ready to rush reinforcements, under naval protection, to the Philippines in time to prevent their capture. To the Army fell the vital task of holding the base in Manila Bay until the arrival of the Fleet, but the major role in any war with Japan would be played by the Navy, for success in the final analysis depended on sea power. War Plan Orange made no provision for a landing on the Japanese home islands. Japan was to be defeated by "isolation and harassment," by the disruption of its vital sea communications, and by "offensive sea and air operations against her naval forces and economic life."

Presumably, it would not be necessary to invade Japan. But the planners recognized that if they could not bring Japan to her knees by these means they would have to take "such further action as may be required to win the war." For about fifteen years, the strategic concepts in the Orange Plan formed the basis for most American war planning. Rarely have plans for a war been so comprehensive and detailed, so complete at every echelon, and so long in preparation. Every conceivable situation that might involve the United States in a war with Japan, including a surprise air attack on Pearl Harbor, was carefully considered and appropriate measures of defense were adopted. At least half a dozen times between 1924 and 1938, the plan was revised, sometimes in response to military changes and sometimes as a result of Congressional sentiment, or because of the international situation. The need for concentration camps for Japanese Americans arose periodically, even by the President himself. Other strategic factors arose.

Japan's increasingly aggressiveness into China particularly worried the US planners. Manchuria was an important region for its rich mineral and coal reserves, and its soil is perfect for soy and barley production. For Japan, Manchuria became an essential source of raw materials. Around the time of World War I, Zhang Zuolin, a former bandit established himself as a powerful warlord with influence over most of Manchuria. He was inclined to keep his Manchu army under his control and to keep Manchuria free of foreign influence. The Japanese tried and failed to assassinate him in 1916. They finally succeeded in June 1928.

Following the Mukden Incident in 1931 and the subsequent Japanese invasion of Manchuria, Inner Manchuria was proclaimed to be Manchukuo, a puppet state under the control of the Japanese army. The last Manchu emperor, Pu yi, was then placed on the throne to lead a Japanese puppet government in the Wei Huang Gong, better known as "Puppet Emperor's Palace." Inner Manchuria was thus detached from China by Japan to create a buffer zone to defend Japan from Russia's Southing Strategy and, with Japanese investment and rich natural resources, became an industrial giant. Under Japanese control, Manchuria was brutally run with a systematic campaign of terror and intimidation against the local Russian and Chinese populations including arrests, organized riots and other forms of subjugation.

The Japanese also began a campaign of emigration to Manchukuo; the Japanese had a plan to bring in 5 million Japanese settlers into Manchukuo and the Japanese population there rose from 240,000 in 1931 to 837,000 in 1939. Hundreds of Manchu farmers were evicted and their farms given to Japanese immigrant -families. Manchukuo was used as a base to invade the rest of China in 1937–40. The US Army and Navy watched with growing anxiety during the 1930's as Japan acquired control of Manchuria, seized strategic points on the north China coast, and denied access to the mandated islands. The Japanese government acted with growing confidence, in the belief that the United States, the Soviet Union, and the European colonial powers were not likely to take concerted action against its expansion.

In 1933 the Japanese government exhibited this confidence by withdrawing from the League of Nations in the face of the Assembly's refusal to recognize the Japanese puppet regime in Manchuria. Having taken this step with impunity, the Japanese government served notice, in accordance with the 1922 treaty terms, of its intention to withdraw from the 1922 and 1930 naval limitations agreements, both of which accordingly expired in 1936. By the mid-1930's, the American military planners had finally concluded that Japan could be defeated only in a long, costly war, in which the Philippines would be lost early, and in which American offensive operations would take the form of a "progressive movement" through the mandated islands, beginning with the Marshalls and Carolines, to establish "a secure line of communications to the Western Pacific."

The planners then faced the question of whether the makers of national policy meant to run the risk and incur the obligation of engaging in such a war. The State Department had not relaxed its opposition to Japanese expansion on the Asiatic continent. This opposition, for which there was a good deal of popular support, involved an ever-present risk of armed conflict. After the passage of the Philippine Independence Act in 1934, the belief gained ground in the War Department that the United states should not run the risk nor incur the obligation of fighting the Japanese in the western Pacific. When the question finally came up in the fall of 1931, the Army planners took the position that the United States should no longer remain liable for a fruitless attempt to defend and relieve the Philippines and the costly attempt to retake them. The senior Army planner, General Stanley D. Embick, stated the case as follows: "If we adopt as our peace-time frontier in the Pacific the line Alaska-Hawaii-Panama: a. Our vital interests will be invulnerable. b. In the wont of war with Japan we will be free to conduct our military (including naval) operations in a manner that will promise success instead of national disaster."

This view was entirely unacceptable to the Navy planners. The whole structure of the Navy's peacetime planning rested on the proposition that the fleet must be ready to take the offensive in the Pacific should war break out. It was out of the question for the Navy planners to agree to give up planning offensive operations west of Hawaii. For two years, the Army and Navy planners engaged in intermittent dispute over the military policy on which they should base plans for fighting a war with Japan. The Chief of Staff of the Army, General Malin Craig, evidently shared the views of his planners, but he was either unable or unwilling to have the dispute brought before the President for decision.

The weakness of the American position in the Far Fast and the danger of war steadily became more apparent. The expiration of the naval limitations agreements re-opened the possibility that the United States might fortify Guam, thus partially neutralizing the Japanese position in its mandates (which were presumably being fortified, since it had become impossible to gain access to them or much intelligence about them). The Congress refused to authorize this step. In the summer of 1937 the Japanese began an undeclared war in China—the "China Incident"—bringing closer the moment at which the United States must choose either to accept or oppose Japanese aims.

The planners finally came to an agreement by avoiding the disputed issues. Early in 1938 they submitted a revised plan, which the Joint Board, the Chief of Staff, and the Chief and Secretaries of Naval Operations approved. The Navy planners agreed to eliminate references to an offensive war, the mission of destroying Japanese forces, and the early movement of the fleet into the western Pacific in return for the agreement that the Army planners would eliminate the proviso that any operations west of Midway would require the specific authorization of the President. The revised plan gave no indication of how long it should take the Navy to advance into the western Pacific and tacitly recognized the hopeless position of the American forces in the Philippines. Those forces retained the basic mission "to hold the entrance to Manila Bay, to deny Manila Bay to Orange [Japanese] naval forces," with little hope of reinforcement.

The version of the Navy's Orange War Plan which was current in 1941 actually had its inception in May 1929 as WPL13; it changed eight times in ten years. Orange number six, in May 1937, brought the

Navy's plan into line with the Joint Army-Navy Basic War Plan Orange. It is both interesting and instructive to follow the ups and downs of (WPL13) from 1937 to 1941, since they provide a revealing insight into the events at Pearl Harbor on December 7, 1941. The basic feature of WPL13 in 1937 was a U.S. Navy offensive into the western Pacific from Pearl Harbor. The initial objective of this operation was to either relieve the defenders of Manila Bay or recapture it. Although the Army thought the offensive aspects of this Orange plan in 1937 were "an act of madness," they could not argue that Manila Bay was the best and possibly the only base from which to conduct future offensive operations in support of other US interests in the Far East. Here was an obvious area for future compromises.

The Navy Base War Plan Orange for 1938 contained three new assumptions inspired by extensive Army revisions to the Joint Plan, which eliminated all references to offensive warfare: (1) outbreak of war would be preceded by a period of strained relations; (2) Orange would attack without warning; and (3) a superior US fleet would operate west of Hawaii. The eighth and final change to WPL13 was made in March 1939. This change reflected the initial shift in US strategic thinking from the Pacific to events in Europe and the Atlantic Ocean, away from offensive operations toward a concept of defensive operations and readiness. At the same time, a new planning system replaced the colors adopted over thirty years with the Rainbow Plans.

Until 1939, the US government followed a pattern of conflicting policies regarding China and Japan. Committed on the one hand to an Open Door Policy toward China, the US conversely recognized in 1908 and again in 1917 that Japan had special rights and interest in eastern Asia because of its "territorial propinquity." The Lansing-Ishii Agreement of 1917, in fact, specifically recognized Japan's special position in Manchuria and on the Shantung Peninsula. Moreover, until 1941 the US consistently supplied Japan with the war materials necessary to undertake and sustain operations not only against China but against the Netherlands and France as well. At the same time, the United States maintained a naval rivalry with Japan which, because of various factors, had already begun to tilt in Japan's favor following the end of World War I.

As the war in Europe expanded and Japanese behavior toward China, the United States, England, and France grew more intransigent, a realization developed in Navy circles that budgetary decisions since the end of World War I, and particularly since 1929, had almost crippled the U.S. fleet. The most severe suffering was felt in manpower-intensive activities. While German and Japan openly rebuilt their military during the depression years, the US Congress, preoccupied with disarmament and rebuilding the nation's economy, consistently placed harsh fiscal constraints on the Navy. In the name of disarmament, Congress called for reductions in both capital expenditures and manpower. Forced by domestic economic considerations to cut back on military spending, the US continued to adhere to arms limitations agreements and self-imposed building moratoriums well into the 1930s while the Axis powers skillfully circumvented them by modernization programs and new construction. By 1939 both the U.S. and British navies had fallen behind the Japanese Navy, not just in numbers of modern vessels but particularly in the technology of naval architecture and armaments, ship design, hull speeds, torpedoes, and the caliber of ships' guns.

The latest revision of these plans, completed in April 1941 and called War Plan Orange-3, was based on the joint Army-Navy Orange plan of 1938, one of the many "color" plans developed during the prewar years. Each color plan dealt with a different situation, Orange covering an emergency in which only the United States and Japan would be involved. In this sense, the plan was strategically unrealistic and completely outdated by 1941. Tactically, however, the plan was an excellent one and its provisions for defense were applicable under any local situation.

In War Plan Orange, it was assumed that the Japanese attack would come without a declaration of war and with less than forty-eight hours' warning so that it would not be possible to provide reinforcements from the United States for some time. The defense would therefore have to be conducted entirely by the military and naval forces already in the Philippines, supported by such forces as were available locally. The last category included any organized elements of the Philippine Army which might be inducted into the service of the United States under the Philippine Independence Act. An analysis of Japanese capabilities, as of July 1, 1940, led the Philippine Department planners to believe that the enemy would send an expedition of about 100,000 men to capture Manila and its harbor defenses in order to occupy the Philippines, sever the American line of communications, and deny the United States a naval base in the Far East. The attack would probably come during the dry season, shortly after the rice crop was harvested, in December or January. The enemy was assumed to have extensive knowledge of the terrain and of American strength and dispositions, and would probably be assisted by the 30,000 Japanese in the Islands. Army planners in the Philippines expected the Japanese to make their major attack against the island of Luzon and to employ strong ground forces with heavy air and naval support. They would probably land in many places simultaneously in order to spread thin the defending forces and assure the success of at least one of the landings. Secondary landings or feints were also expected. It was considered possible that the Japanese might attempt in a surprise move to seize the harbor defenses with a small force at the opening of hostilities. Enemy air operations would consist of long-range reconnaissance and bombardment, probably coming without warning and coordinated with the landings. The Japanese would probably also attempt to establish air bases on Luzon very early in the campaign in order to destroy American air power and bomb military installations.

Under WPO-3 the mission of the Philippine garrison was to hold the entrance to Manila Bay and deny its use to Japanese naval forces. There was no intention that American troops should fight anywhere but in central Luzon. US Army forces, constituting the Initial Protective Force, had the main task of preventing enemy landings. Failing in this, they were to defeat those forces which succeeded in landing. If, despite these attempts, the enemy proved successful, the Initial Protective Force was to engage in delaying action but not at the expense of the primary mission—the defense of Manila Bay. Every attempt was to be made to hold back the Japanese advance while withdrawing to the Bataan peninsula. Bataan was recognized as the key to the control of Manila Bay, and it was to be defended to the "last extremity."

Nothing was said in WPO-3 about what was to happen after the defenses on Bataan crumbled. Presumably by that time, estimated at six months, the US Pacific Fleet would have fought its way across the Pacific, won a victory over the Combined Fleet, and made secure the line of communications. The men and supplies collected on the west coast during that time would then begin to reach the Philippines in a steady stream. The Philippine garrison, thus reinforced, could then counterattack and drive the enemy into the sea.

Actually, no one in a position of authority at that time (April 1941) believed that anything like this would happen. Informed naval opinion estimated that it would require at least two years for the Pacific Fleet to fight its way across the Pacific. There was no plan to concentrate men and supplies on the West Coast and no schedule for their movement to the Philippines. Army planners in early 1941 believed that at the end of six months, if not sooner, supplies would be exhausted and the garrison would go down in defeat. WPO-3 did not say this; instead it said nothing at all. And everyone hoped that when the time came something could be done, some plan improvised to relieve or rescue the men stranded 7,000 miles across the Pacific.

CHAPTER 2

A Businessman in New York City

Hideo moved to New York City in 1918 and established his own company specializing in hand-painted silk lampshades, but went bankrupt at the time of the Great Depression, a year before the birth of his daughter Yoshiko Joy. Recovering quickly, both financially and emotionally, the resilient Issei found employment with a Japanese import-export company in 1930. Hideo liked the best of clothing, selecting clothes from the finest department stores in New York. Joy recalls that her father had a cane, not because of a physical disability but because it complemented his fine clothes. His hats were the best he could find. His cane was fitted with a diamond in the handle. He was a dashing figure in the finest clothes.

Hideo met Fusako Ikeda during 1926. They were married in 1928. Fusako arrived in New York as a tourist, in 1926 with her younger sister, Michiko and her husband, Tsunezo Tanaka, to live near their older sister, Muneko and her husband, Toshio Tobita, who had arrived in New York City before 1920. Although living in separate apartments, the three families spent a great deal of time together. Toshio Tobita had his own watch crystal company in Manhattan, Hideo worked for a Japanese trading company in New York City, and Tsunezo Tanaka, a University of Michigan graduate, was a fur broker. Fusako had arrived after the passage of America's notorious Japanese Exclusion Act of 1924. In order to stay in New York when her tourist visa expired, she attended Mitchell Designing School from which she graduated and worked as a fashion designer. Shortly after her marriage, she and her husband traveled to Toronto, Canada, so that she could re-enter the U.S. on a non-tourist visa, allowing a form of permanent residency.

They lived contentedly until, at the time of the U.S. presidential election in 1940, the Japanese business community in New York City concluded that if Franklin Delano Roosevelt became re-elected, it would mean a war between Japan and the US. Japan's consular officials apparently provided the businesses with advisories that FDR's policies and intentions were extremely hostile. As a result, beginning in January 1941, family members of employees in Japanese companies in New York City began returning to Japan. Their companies strongly encouraged them to do so. Hideo agreed that his wife, Fusako, should return to Japan and she should be accompanied by their daughter Yoshiko Joy. Mother and daughter departed New York City on January 12, 1941, by train for the West Coast and then by ship to Yokohama, arriving February 4, 1941. Hideo remained working in New York City.

An American youth in Japan for the first time, Yoshiko Joy began a new life , enduring all the deprivations and surviving life-threatening hazards of the Japanese. These included fire-bombings and P-51 strafing of civilians. She witnessed and survived the fire bombings of Tokyo that killed thousands. Joy explained:

> I do want to tell you a few recollections of that time when we lived in constant dread of the air raids (*kuushuu*) in Tokyo. The warning sirens were throughout the city. They blasted out from each ward office (*kuyakusho*) or each building that had a siren installed. The air raid warning signal was a series of long blasts but the 'take cover because the planes are overhead' signals were the short siren blasts, repeated and repeated and repeated. Believe it or not I broke out in goose pimples for at least 20 years after the war ended, each time I heard a siren, any place. To this day, more than 65 years later, sirens still remind me of the air raids, but I am no longer fearful.
>
> The March 10, 1945 Tokyo air raid was the beginning of the frequent, it seemed like daily, air raids, with mostly incendiary bombs (*shoidan*) rather than explosive bombs (*bakudan*). The bombings on March 10, focused on downtown Tokyo around Nihonbashi, Asakusa, Sumida River area, all of the old Edo Shitamachi area. From where we lived in Meguro, we could see the entire sky from horizon upward into the sky as far as the eye could see, all ablaze in orange-red colors. We could hear the

sound of bombs, recognizable from the sound of 'bombing' in movies. Edo completely burned through the night with untold numbers of scorched, dead people.

What was reported and confirmed by several people I have met who were among the few that survived was that the B-29s dropped the firebombs in concentric circles starting from the outer side going round and round (dropping firebombs) toward the center. The only way of escape, at least for those in the outer circle areas (early on as the bombings started) was to run toward and into the fire circle (avoiding the individual fires the best you could). One man, now living in Nihonbashi, told me that he knew right away that if you tried to run away from the fires you would end up at the river with no place to go, you just had to run into and toward where it was coming from in order to escape.

He tried to tell all his neighbors to run with him and his wife with two small children toward the fires and not away from the fires toward the river. Only the very few who followed him survived the attack. He said psychologically it is difficult to run toward, instead of away from, the fires and the enemy knew that and that is why they bombed in concentric circle patterns starting from the outer rim in. A few days after that horrific air raid, he walked into and around the area he had run away from. Unfortunately, most people ran into the inferno. Burnt black bodies were everywhere. People who tried to escape the flames by standing and huddling against the concrete wall of a theater that was near the river were scorched black and still standing. The heat apparently was so intense that the people were totally scorched before they fell. Hard to believe, but that's what he saw. Many people, trying to flee the fires, but no place to go, jumped into the Sumida River. The surface of the river was entirely covered with human bodies.

Shortly after the Tokyo Shitamachi area bombings, the B-29s started coming over our area, Shibuya, Meguro, and Ohmori. Air raids were usually at night. We all could recognize B-29s from the wing lights. Toshio Tsuzuki (my husband) said one time he figured if he stood near the large wall next to the Meguro Ward office building (he knew which side the B-29s would come from), he would have less chance of being hit by a fire bomb. They came whizzing down in canisters, like closed umbrellas, spewing out their jelly balls of fire. When Toshio realized that the four-engine B-29 was flying in so low that he could actually see the silhouette of the pilot, he started running as fast as he could, as if trying to outrun the plane that was chasing him. He kept his head turned looking at the pilot while running until he crashed into a tree. It sounds hilarious now, but at the time he was dead serious running for his life. Toshio still remembers how much the collision with the tree hurt. He managed to run home only to find the *engawa* (veranda) of his house on fire. He was able to put that fire out with pails of water from the big tub of water that was kept for these emergencies. When the firebombs start raining down, Toshio says he figured that to lay on the ground increased one's target area so he always stood vertically, sometimes spinning around, to minimize the space he occupied.

In fact, another of his close-call, scary experiences was during the daytime air raid on August 10, 1945, less than a week before Japan's surrender was announced. Toshio, being a university chemistry student, was assigned to work at the Hodogaya Chemical Company located near the Sumida River where many industrial companies were located. The employees heard over the loudspeaker warnings to enter the closest bomb shelter immediately because that industrial area was being targeted by heavy bombing. The only 'bomb shelter' available was an above ground shelter, since ground level was too low, near the river to dig shelters underground. As they crowded into the shelter, Toshio said he felt sure that it was the end for him, and that he was going to die in the shelter. They heard and felt a tremendous explosion followed by a huge gust of wind that blew into the shelter. At that moment, Toshio knew they had survived the bombing because it was not a direct hit. Had the bomb hit the shelter, they would have all been killed.

Joy added:

I remember hearing a strange roar that kept getting louder. It was like a whizzing, deafening roar. I slid into a covered trench that we had made in our yard, just in time, not a fraction of a second too late. The sound was that of a fire bomb hurtling to the ground. It dug itself into the ground where I had been standing just before I slid into the trench. A few jelly balls of fire (napalm) sprayed out, but nothing happened. At our neighbor's, the firebomb came through the roof and landed on the futon under which the man was sleeping. He jumped up, and seeing the tiny flames all over his futon, he panicked and, instead of smothering the flames, he shook the futon intending to shake away the flames. What happened instead was that all those jelly balls were flung all over the room and onto the walls which caused a major fire. That's what those firebombs are intended to do!

By early summer 1945, it was not only B-29s coming at night to drop firebombs, but the single engine P-51s started coming to strafe people on the ground. I clearly remember seeing them. I was on my way home with a backpack full of sugar, an extremely rare commodity which I was able to get from a farmer in the mountains. Apparently, the farmer had been placed in charge of a storage shed used by the Imperial Household Agency. It was through 'confidential' arrangements that I would be able to make a special barter. The conditions required me to be alone, without an adult, and that I had to deliver a backpack full of girl's clothes. I would be given sugar in exchange. I had lots of clothes from New York City and quite happy to make such an exchange. Needless to say, at home, that sugar could be used to exchange for other kinds of food. Really, sugar was invaluable at that time.

At any rate, in order to get to this farmhouse and shed, I had a 40-minute ride by train and then a two hour hike up the mountain side, including wading across a stream. The sugar seemed to weigh a ton, but I think it was about 15 kg. I pretty much wobbled down the mountain side, across the stream and got to the rice paddy area not far from the train station when I heard the plane. I could hardly run with the heavy load on my back, but was able to get under a tree, the only place to hide. I could clearly see the face of the pilot in the cockpit of the small P-51. He flew down low over the rice paddies and strafed only women, because all working men were away from home 'in the service of their country.' What amazed me is that those bullets streaming out of the plane are visible as streaks (tracers) just like they are drawn in comic strips. That's the only place I had seen strafing before.

My guess is the pilot was on his way back after his 'mission' whatever it was and just wanted to get rid of his leftover ammunition so he swooped down and strafed whatever it was below him. War reduces human life to that level? I was terrified standing under the tree. The pilot could see just as clearly as the people scurrying around on the ground. He knew that most of his targets were women. The life or death question for me was whether to leave my back pack of sugar and run for my life to the train station, or hang on to the sugar and wobble to the train station hoping to not get strafed en route. I just could not bear to leave the sugar, not because I wanted to eat anything sweet, but because I was acutely aware how that sugar would transform into many things for my family and even friends, too. Luckily I did get safely home with the precious sugar.

There are other experiences of war Joy encountered, but we must now return to Hideo's travails. Adventurousness and daring characterized his life whether in Japan or in the United States. Most notably, he could not be brought to anger in unfair, discriminatory situations. In the United States, when Pearl Harbor was attacked on December 7, 1941, Hideo was on a business trip away from his home office in New York City and staying at a hotel in Miami, Florida. That night, around midnight, two well-prepared FBI agents came to his hotel room and told him he was under arrest as an enemy alien which surprised him. It was an outlandish accusation. Because of discriminatory laws he had been forced to remain an alien—he could not become a U.S. citizen. He had been a law-abiding resident of America for over 35 years. Hideo had not protested his years of unfair treatment; he had committed no offense—not even a parking violation. It was an unfair accusation and arrest in the extreme.

Hideo belonged to a private Japanese club in New York, called Toyokan, where parties were held, and socializing occurred. The FBI concluded that spying MUST have occurred there if fishermen, grocers, labor union officials, cooks, and bakers of the Tokyo social syndicate were agents. The FBI were determined to find spies and saboteurs among the Japanese Americans, even though none existed. Another Issei, Otoichi Nishimoto, living in rural Hood River, Oregon, was arrested by the FBI for having one .22 caliber cartridge. When Otoichi surrendered his shotgun, rifle, and ammunition to authorities immediately after December 7, 1941, he had overlooked one cartridge. He was quickly taken into custody in December 1941 and sent to a detention center in Missoula, Montana. After six months in prison, he was released and returned to Hood River in time to join his family in their detention on May 13, 1942 in Pinedale Assembly Center, near Fresno, California.

Working under the assumptions of War Plan Orange and his power of Presidential leadership, as early as August 10, 1936, Franklin Delano Roosevelt had secretly ordered the preparation of concentration camps for Americans of Japanese ancestry in the United States. Concentration camps normally are a corollary of wars. They are for captured enemy soldiers in wars. So, why was the imprisoning order for U.S. citizens and residents, who were noncombatants? One must consider that FDR was part of those, along with John L. DeWitt, who developed War Plan Orange. FDR also worked with the US intelligence agencies who saw nothing different between people living in the Japanese archipelago and American citizens of Japanese descent.

Following Japan's attack on Pearl Harbor in 1941, concerns about subversive activity by Japanese Americans grew more pressing. Office of Naval Intelligence (ONI) commissioned Kenneth Ringle, assistant district intelligence officer for the Eleventh Naval District in Los Angeles, to conduct a thorough investigation of the resident Japanese population. He found little evidence of Japanese American saboteurs, and in his final report to President Roosevelt, advised against mass incarceration, a view that was shared by most ONI officials, but that was largely ignored by the Army and War Department. It is readily seen that good sense was ignored and emotional motivations were most important.

Law enforcement and intelligence agencies began manufacturing—creating—a "nest-full of spies." Their secret assessments, now declassified, show that socially successful Japanese in the U.S. were preyed upon for these purposes.

The secret Office of Naval Intelligence report on the "Japanese Tokyo Club Syndicate with interlocking affiliations," December 24, 1941, shows the distorted intelligence operations necessary for defense against espionage when none existed at all. U.S. authorities negotiating prisoner of war exchanges with Japan had the problem of "finding" enemy Japanese nationals to exchange. So, simply stated, they were conveniently manufactured. Fair minded readers will conclude that the formerly secret ONI report remained hidden from public scrutiny until 1985 to conceal the facts of lives disrupted and destroyed to maintain false assumptions of intelligence skill.

The Office of Naval Intelligence is a military intelligence agency of the United States Navy. Established in 1882 to advance the Navy's modernization efforts, ONI is the oldest organization in the United States intelligence community and has served as the premier source of maritime intelligence. Since World War I, its mission was broadened to include real-time reporting on the developments and activities of foreign navies; protecting maritime resources and interests; monitoring and countering transnational maritime threats; providing operational and tactical support to the U.S. Navy and its partners; and surveying the global maritime environment. During the 1920s and 1930s, many of ONI's activities were dedicated to Japan, which was analyzed as an increasingly advanced and belligerent naval power. Because Japan had provided very important naval support to Britain during World War I, the office investigated Japanese fortifications in the Pacific, acquired information on Japanese military aircraft and weaponry, and partnered with the U.S. Army's Military Intelligence Division and the Federal Bureau of Investigation to monitor what was thought to be subversive elements in the American Japanese community. This persistent need for investigating subversive activity in America—when none existed in the Japanese community—reveals management biases and, if one is to be generous, policy emphasis. ONI's director met weekly with his counterparts in FBI and military intelligence to share information on suspected internal threats. In 1929, Chief of Naval Operations William D. Leahy made permanent ONI's functions as an intelligence office, while in 1939, President Franklin D. Roosevelt granted the office considerable authority on matters of domestic security.

With such a respected record, it is disappointing to find evidence of dismal security checks of Japanese Americans. The secret US intelligence report on the "Japanese Tokyo Club Syndicate with Interlocking Affiliations," prepared by the Counter-Subversion Section of the Office of Naval Intelligence on December 24, 1941, was such a distortion of facts on Japanese Americans that their lives were changed. Yet, until its declassification on May 14, 1985, its validity was not questioned. It found extensive subversive activity among ethnic Japanese in the Western hemisphere when none existed. With the sudden outbreak of hostilities between Japan and the United States on December 7, 1941, an extensive program for the "detention of enemy aliens" was put into operation. Having been under surveillance for years, hundreds of allegedly dangerous suspects were rounded up.

Understandably, official government representatives of the Axis Powers were put under surveillance or taken into custody. Enemy alien hearing boards were appointed to inquire into the activities and loyalty of the individuals concerned. Other less rational steps were taken. The simplest step—among the less effective means—was to search for anyone "looking like the enemy." Aided by intelligence recommendations, the U.S. Attorney General decided whether an alien or citizen was to be interned for the duration of the war, be released unconditionally, or paroled. This detention and internment of Japanese Americans resulted in innocent resident aliens and American citizens eventually becoming transferred to Japan as prisoners of war.

To worsen the imaginary threat, these arbitrary rules were applied to ethnic Japanese anywhere in the Western Hemisphere, except in those nations which had been historically aggrieved by the US, which refused to cooperate. Unfortunately, other countries did. Without proof, ethnic Japanese were kidnapped out of such places as Peru, the Panama Canal Zone, and Honduras, branded as agents of Japan, and sent to Japan as prisoners of war. Most of these innocent men, women, and children were uprooted, imprisoned, and shipped off to a foreign land. Beginning in 1942, the United States seized 2,264 men women and children of Japanese ancestry from 12 countries in Latin America, of which 80 percent were Peruvian. They were shipped to detention centers in Panama and in several states of the United States. The forced abduction, internment, treatment, and exchanges of these persons constituted gross violations of humanitarian law at that time, and though the United Nations has taken up the sordid violation of rights, no resolution is in sight. The surviving Latin American Japanese were excluded in the program carried out by the United States to compensate American Japanese for their internment in camps and other related damages, and therefore suffer discrimination.

We have documents provided by the Japanese Peruvian Oral History Project that fully describe these events. The Project seeks the support of a Sub-Commission and interested non-governmental organizations. One of the kidnapped victims tells the harrowing story:

> I was born in Lima, Peru. My parents owned a business importing textiles and making dress shirts to sell to retail stores. My maternal grandparents owned a department store and were among the first to be arrested and used in a hostage exchange. After that first time that a US Army transport took away Japanese Peruvians, whenever US Army transports would come into Callao harbor, some men would go into hiding, including my father. The police came to our house looking for my father several times. The final time, again not finding him, they arrested my mother and put her in jail for two days. My sister, who was 11, went with her because she did not want our mother to go alone. When my father learned of this, he immediately came out of hiding and my mother and sister were released.
>
> Our family was brought to the US on the US Army transport Cuba, guarded by American military personnel, who were armed with rifles, machine guns and whips. As we boarded the ship, we were searched. On orders of the US government, all passports and visas were confiscated. Families were separated on the ship. The women and children were put into small cabins. I was only 13, but was put below deck with the men. We were only allowed to go on deck twice a day for ten minutes and were never allowed to see our families. We had to endure these overcrowded conditions for 21 days. From Callao to New Orleans, the ship was guarded by US destroyers and submarines.
>
> In New Orleans, the women and children were led off the ship first. They were marched straight to a warehouse, where they were forced to strip and stand in line naked. Then they were sprayed with insecticide. My sister, who was only 11, said she could never forget how humiliated she felt, having been

> forced to strip in front of boys and felt sorry for the mothers, who were very modest. The men, then went through the same process. After we all showered, we boarded a train. During the train ride to Crystal City, Texas, we were ordered to keep the shades down the entire two days. My sister thought we were all going to be killed at the end of the train ride.
>
> We were kept in an internment camp in Crystal City for two and a half years. My father had us attend Japanese school in the internment camp. He thought it would be more useful when we returned to Peru because English was rarely spoken there. In the summer of 1946, there were reports that the internment camp was going to be closed and that we would be deported because we were considered illegal aliens. Our family wanted to return to Peru, but the Peruvian government would not allow us to return. So, we were paroled to Seabrook Farms in New Jersey.

Years after peace arrangements of World War II, the former resident Americans (citizens) and Latin Americans who survived the war had to find their way back to Central and South America and the United States. Some did; some were unable to do so, and lived in limbo. Some died as innocent casualties of war. The fate of these Japanese residents had been sealed by intelligence reports such as that on the Tokyo Club Syndicate, which because of its wide applicability and identification of individuals as spies, remained classified and hidden from public view until 1985. It mattered little that it contained gross distortions of fact. As a result, some US citizens remain forcefully removed from America, labeled as Japanese citizens, abandoned, and forgotten.

The declassified report is quoted in part to convey the sweeping conclusions made. Once such false statement reported that:

> Although handicapped by the detention of many of its key individuals, the Japanese Intelligence Network in this hemisphere continues in operation. Recent reports have been received of suspicious movements of Japanese in various parts of Latin America, particularly in Mexico. On December 13th, one vessel of the Japanese fishing fleet, the ALERT, which was captured off Costa Rica by a Navy Air Patrol, was found to be carrying

> some 10,000 gallons of diesel fuel oil. The ship, Alert, of American registry, is partly owned and manned by Japanese. At the time of her capture, it is believed she was headed for a rendezvous with an enemy submarine or surface raider.

Another claimed that "Isolated as these instances may appear to be, they are actually integral parts of a comprehensive hemispheric intelligence program which the Japanese have been developing for well over a year." The reports assert that "the Japanese Government would intensify the espionage activities of their non-political agencies in this country, relaxing their former policy of 'cultural enlightenment and propaganda.'" ONI's accusations grow increasingly improbable:

> From sources in Mexico have come numerous rumors that approximately five thousand Japanese are congregating at some undetermined point in strategic Baja California. In this connection, one hundred of a Japanese population of six hundred in and around Ensenada, recently left the region in a ship which had been anchored off the coast. Moreover, during the night of December 10, 1941, all Japanese nationals living in Tijuana disappeared, apparently because of a report that the Mexican Government was recruiting Chinese for their armed forces. Those Japanese who remain are observed to be closely associated with Italians in the vicinity...
>
> The Japanese practice of cloaking subversive operations with 'legitimate business fronts' exists in Mexico as well as in the United States. Late in November, 1941, it was reported that Saburo Yoshitaki, a button manufacturer of San Luis (near Mexicali) had installed short wave radio transmitting and receiving sets in his factory and that all of the Japanese in the surrounding district came there to listen. He is also believed to be connected with radio station KEY in Yuma, Arizona, and is considered potentially dangerous.

CHAPTER 3

Betrayal

Sadly, ONI was improperly used by FDR in the days prior to WWII. Japanese Americans who profitably operated businesses or were prominent for social reasons became victims of this analysis. No one was more successful than Hideo Okamoto. He was selected for prisoner of war exchange even though he was not in the employ of the Japanese government. Nevertheless, officials of the US government supporting FDR's order for war focused their attention on Hideo and others of prominence in the Japanese communities. Having been pre-selected, Hideo was picked up, arrested, and detained by the FBI immediately on December 7, 1941 when he was working temporarily in Miami from New York. Though he was not even in his home territory but a Florida hotel room, the FBI had pursued and arrested him immediately on Pearl Harbor day. And, if he really had been a secret agent of Japan, the U.S. government would have put him on trial in the U.S. It could not bring him to a court because he was no more a spy than Cinderella.

For nearly 40 years, Hideo had been a model citizen in communities in California and New York committing no crime and caring for his family. He had a better-than-normal education in America and preached no angry themes against persons or governments. Yet, he was arrested on an imagined political crime, which is not difficult to see from the wildly imaginative analysis of the Japanese community made in secret by the law enforcement and intelligence authorities of the U.S. government.

Not ever provoked into anger, Hideo was always of good humor and of even disposition. Even though he was a friendly Issei, however, he was not to be pushed around. He told the FBI agents that he never goes out without first taking a shower. So they told him to take his shower. Hideo explained to his family much later that he took the longest shower he could. When he finished, he found that the FBI agents had already packed his suitcase; he objected and told them he had a special way of packing and did not like the way they packed "HIS" suitcase. They let him completely repack his belongings. He was obviously stalling for time, but they obliged. By then, it was almost dawn so Hideo asked if they would wait until his dry cleaner opened because he had two Palm Beach suits there that he wanted to pick up. They responded, however, that he would not need Palm Beach suits in jail and they would not wait any longer.

He got into their car to be taken to the Miami Police Station, but en route he asked if they might stop at a diner because he was very hungry and would like to have breakfast. He offered to treat the two FBI men to breakfast. They did stop at a diner so that Hideo could have breakfast, but would not let him treat them. They drank coffee at a separate table—near the exit where they could watch Hideo—while he leisurely ate his breakfast. Hideo said throughout the entire encounter with these two FBI agents, they were polite and respectful.

At the police station, Hideo was told he was under arrest as an enemy alien and was put in jail. He said the jail door closed electrically; the warden shouted "All heads in," and if the prisoners did not withdraw their heads, they would be crushed. He was in a cell by himself. The food was brought to him in a metal pail ("mushy slop" he called it) and the keeper used a metal spoon to literally throw the slop onto his metal plate. He did not eat that unmentionable food for the first few days because the warden told him that prisoners could purchase candy bars from a sales stand in the jail using whatever money they had in their wallets before they were arrested. Hideo asked the warden to bring him candy bars while his money lasted, but eventually had to eat the prison slop.

After two or three months in jail, until the early spring of 1942, authorities transferred Hideo to a concentration camp in Tennessee, possibly in Crossville, which was called "the Jap Camp." Hideo thought he was the only Issei detained there since he saw no other Japanese. This "camp" also held many German businessmen who happened to be in the U.S. when the war broke out. They were not U.S. residents; they were German visitors stranded in the U.S. They were very useful for the U.S. government in these arbitrary prisoner exchanges.

Under house arrest at different locations, such as Homestead Hotel, Hot Springs, Virginia, with much better accommodations than city jails, Ambassadors Kichisaburo Nomura and Saburo Kurusu, Japanese diplomats, and businessmen were also to be placed aboard the ship. Only these Japanese diplomats, those accredited to the United States as Japan's representatives including military attaches, were among those members in the first exchange who could legally and legitimately be called prisoners of war. Hideo Okamoto was an innocent, upstanding resident in New York. He was not a prisoner of war nor was he a criminal. But the FBI treated him as both. To add insult to injury, he had no legal recourse and was compelled to abide by arbitrary, outrageous "application of law." And he did not get angry.

The absurdity of Hideo's story was merely the beginning. Under the guise of returning diplomatic families home in time of war—ostensibly a nice act—an outrage was transpiring. Women and children became pawns in the prisoner of war exchange. It needs repeating, they were prisoners of war—entire families, long-time residents of America, having had nothing to do with the government of Japan. Like many U.S. government actions taken against Japanese residents in the United States, they were hostile, government-supported plans of long-standing origin.

Research in the personal data shown in a Japanese language document written by the inmates, the prisoners themselves in Crystal City, Texas, revealed that many families were native residents of Hawaii and California, not military members of the armed forces of Japan. Other Japanese residents were abducted from Central and South America. Unless they chose otherwise, American citizens should have remained in the United States—their home. Of course, they did not even belong in the U.S. concentration camps established by Executive Order 9066. Instead, in another violation of basic democratic principles, American citizens were sent to Japan in a prisoner of war exchange as Japanese citizens. They were no more nationals of Japan than Lt. General John L. DeWitt who despised them as he said, "a Jap is a Jap, whether a US citizen or not."

All sensible people are shocked at travesties of justices. I am irate because the first prisoner of war exchange ship—*kokansen*—with enemy Japan in 1942 had Nisei children, little American children, aboard as "Japanese prisoners of war." It was an outrageous, unconscionable ploy. All those boarding the exchange ship, SS *Gripsholm*, were identified as Japanese prisoners of war. They were railroaded because there were no real, honest-to-goodness prisoners of war in the U.S. to exchange. Instead, the criterion for a prisoner of war was simply looking Japanese.

So, Hideo and others the U.S. government wanted to get rid of were arbitrarily selected and disposed of. To make these distortions possible in its fraudulent December 24, 1941 analysis, ONI asserted that "Japanese nationals and pro-Japanese Nisei who are well settled in normal and yet strategic occupations are likely to be the mainstay of Japanese espionage-sabotage operations in this country."

Thus it labeled those with ties to Japanese organizations to be inimical to American interests. One such man was American-born Japanese Hoshi Hiroshi (Paul), who, in 1933, was reported to be the president of the Seattle Japanese Amateur Radio Club and an operator of Station W7CFJ, and four years later, was claimed to run a fishing boat out of San Diego. Another was Susumu Hasuike, reported in 1940 to be the owner of Three Star Produce Company in Los Angeles, California, and a member of the suspect Sakura Kai (Cherry Blossom Society), and to have donated $1,000 to the equally suspect Nippon Kaigun Kyokai (The Japan Naval Society). Also a George Takigawa was under suspicion because, as a delegate to the National Convention of the American Federation of Labor, Alaska Cannery Workers Union, he was reported to be associated with the "Association of Japanese Cannery Workers which aims to consolidate the Japanese elements into a united labor front."

The Office of Naval Intelligence warned:

> It is obvious that the Japanese are in control of key positions and have utilized the union as a front for activities far removed from the demands of normal cannery business... [and] that the union's connections with the West Coast Japanese consulates, Army and Navy agents, officials of the Tokyo Club chain, and other suspects have been more than coincidental. It must constantly be kept in mind in this connection that Japan strove to put into operation in the United States and its territories a

> highly integrated and specialized intelligence network which could 'take over' from regular established agencies in wartime.

In calmer times, this type of movie script would have been rejected because it lacked realism and believability. Unfortunately, this wildly imaginative advice was taken seriously and law enforcement agencies and the FBI took measures that inflicted serious harm and losses on Issei and Nisei in America. Too many fell in harm's way, were extradited to a devastated Japan, and their lives disrupted in unimaginable ways.

Hideo Okamoto, Joy's railroaded father, was unjustifiably traded as a prisoner of war and forced to live out his life in Japan. The US citizen children exchanged with Hideo, delivered to Japan remain abandoned and forgotten. They have grown up, transplanted and without normality. They are now senior citizens in Japan, but remain abandoned and forgotten by America. We pray that they were fortunate enough to have survived the war.

At the minimum sense of decency, Hideo Okamoto's story must be told and re-told.

Having been arbitrarily selected, arrested, and convicted without benefit of court, all in a matter of a few hours, Hideo was jailed for almost half a year before being transferred to a concentration camp as an enemy, a spy, without a trial by American authorities. Not consumed by anger over false accusations and convictions, Hideo remained confined in Tennessee until June, 1942. His personal losses were huge—three decades of goodwill and personal property, all were lost. On June 18, 1942, with no recourse against the US government, he was placed aboard on the neutral exchange ship, *Gripsholm*, a Swedish liner that sailed from Ellis Island, New York City, as a part of the first exchange of "prisoners of war" with Japan.

In addition, Japanese Latin Americans abducted from Central and South American countries and falsely accused as espionage agents comprised the first "prisoner of war" exchange. The abductions of Japanese Latin Americans from Peru, and brought to the United States had been secretly masterminded by US officials. Approximately 2,300 men, women, and children of Japanese descent from Peru and 11 other Latin American countries were brought to a concentration camp in Crystal City, Texas, and held in the custody of the Immigration and

Naturalization Service from 1941 through 1948. This illegal atrocity was acknowledged and publicly apologized for on June 15, 2011, by Peruvian President Alan Gabriel Ludwig García Pérez. He admitted,

> Mistreatment was given by Peruvian authorities and people to Japanese immigrants and descendants in 1941. Although relations between Peru and Japan are currently friendly and harmonious, they also had serious problems, as in that year, when thousands of Japanese and their children born in Peru were arrested arbitrarily and illegally, deported to the United States and imprisoned . . . many of the deportees did not return, many of the detainees lost their property and businesses and many of them were unable to retrieve their farms and agricultural lands. . . . All this cannot remain in silence as if nothing had happened and . . . I apologize for those who committed these criminal acts because they hurt the relationship between two peoples which have been twinned by migration and the coincidence of their destinations.

Peru President Perez asked the mistreated people to look to the future. The main orchestrator of these abductions, the United States, has not admitted its role in the abductions and its use of the victims as prisoners of war. These abductions and banishment of innocent persons have been swept under the American rug.

A Japanese language pamphlet prepared by Japanese internees in 1943 while at the Crystal City concentration camp lists every family that was extradited on the scheduled exchange ship. It is detailed, listing the family's permanent domicile or honseki (where the Japanese government maintains permanent records of a given family). Those who prepared the pamphlet are likely included in the overall document. All incarcerated families were provided a copy. One copy is in the Imari City Library, Imari City, Saga Prefecture, Japan, donated when the author secured a copy from internee Frank Nagashima. Frank was extremely fortunate to have been able to find his way back to the United States.

The Japanese language document listing the Nikkei prisoners is valuable because of the details of family members. It was prepared by Crystal City concentration camp's "Japanese regional organization," enabling the camp to negotiate, through the Spanish government, some terms of the Geneva agreement. All internees are identified by name, country from which they were displaced, and where they were from in Japan. The "Returnees of Second Exchange Ship departing Crystal City on August 29, 1943," embarking on September 1, 1943, contains 33 families with 130 persons (17 families exiled from Hawaii. The rest if the families were from Panama, Nicaragua, El Salvador, California, and Peru). Most of those listed as repatriating from Hawaii ostensibly appear to be members of the diplomatic staff. The obvious question remains: What happened to those 33 families? Where are they now?

The first exchange was conducted by the U.S. government very hastily and arbitrarily in 1942. Few details are available. With emotions running high from the Pearl Harbor attack, many prisoners of war were arbitrarily selected from the Japanese populations in the western hemisphere. They were not captured in combat operations, but appear to have been rounded up from such locations as the female correctional facility in Seagoville, Texas, a small town of 700 located approximately twenty miles southeast of Dallas. In April 1942, the Immigration and Naturalization Service (INS) appropriated the site and operated an internment camp for "enemy aliens."

Many internees, though not all, were Japanese and Germans deported from Latin America to the United States. In general, females and married couples without children were sent to Seagoville, while men were sent to the internment camp at Kenedy and families with children to the camp at Crystal City (both cities in Texas). The INS closed the Seagoville camp in June 1945, and the facility reverted to a minimum-security federal prison.

In the swift pace of uprooting and custodial detention as prisoners, the lives of U.S. citizen children were altered beyond retrieval. Basic rights were erased. They need to be restored, to be returned or given the opportunity to choose the place of their birthright at all possible. Purpose in life is fundamental and these records help clarify moral uncertainties. In a lucky turn of events, this list of abandoned Nisei, exchanged as alleged prisoners of war during World War II has been conveyed to an understanding vice consul at the U.S. Consulate in Fukuoka City on 24 October 2016. Since the US consulates in Japan have the responsibility for US citizens in Japan, efforts are being undertaken to locate them. The Consul for Management and Consular Affairs, Dominic So, has provided assurances that searches will be undertaken. Although consuls are well-intentioned, the change in Presidential responsibilities on January 20, 2017 will adversely change our search.

This detailed review is of members of the "Second Group of Repatriates from Camp Crystal City." We are compelled to undertake similar research on the first group which was much larger, consisting of about 770 persons. Others included in the outrageous exchange were prisoners in America's concentration camps (publicly mandated under Executive Order 9066, effective February 19, 1942) and those held in contrived arrests in America such as Hideo Okamoto. They were individuals in the community who were successful in occupations, particularly in unique cultural fields. It was as if Japanese Americans were penalized for being leaders in their communities. Of course, leaders are easy to identify. Policemen and would-be vigilantes did not need to scour the underbrush to find them.

Hideo Okamoto wore Palm Beach suits and played golf, particularly notorious for aliens. Like Hideo, none had committed any crime for which they could be prosecuted, but they became prisoners of war eligible for exchange and were transferred to Japan. Many had never been in Japan before and became strangers in their alleged "homeland." Their lives need to be restored and brought back, literally and figuratively, to normalcy in America. Those Nisei abandoned in Japan are likely still there. Who is going to provide them with an opportunity of renewed choice? Those of us who have acquired the knowledge of their kidnapping, transfer to Japan, and abandonment must do what is possible to return them to the United States and be provided restitution and comfort.

This first "exchange" group consisted of 1,421 persons, including those who had been abducted from Peru, Nicaragua, Ecuador, Panama, and Hawaii and incarcerated in Seagoville, and Crystal City, Texas, and other concentration camps. It needs emphasis and repeating. They were abducted, kidnapped, in an international conspiracy—not by individuals—but by incredible plotting and machinations between the governments of the United States, Peru, Panama, and Nicaragua. It had the ring of Nazi Germany's roundup of Jews wherever they might be. Those with a conscience will be outraged.

CHAPTER 4

Hideo Okamoto

Returning to Japan and the *Kanyo* Character

Incredibly, throughout Hideo's ordeal as an exchange prisoner of war, he never got angry. So I could not help but ask Japanese in Japan why the Issei rarely got angry. The answer was surprising and nearly unanimously expressed in terms of *kanyosei*. *Kanyo* is a characteristic of the Japanese personality which is generous enough in meaning to apply to any person who accepts its norms; one of its key traits is a broad, thoughtful understanding of people. Its origins are not clear, but appear to be associated with Buddhist teachings. *Kanyosei* defines the circumstances of magnanimity. For purposes of my experiences with Issei and with Japanese behavior in Japan, it has significant applicability. Japanese conduct in the Meiji and the late Tokugawa periods formed around spiritual generosity. It remains a basic characteristic of the modern Japanese, but is rarely talked about. It is for Japanese to do so.

First, anyone with *kanyo* looks upon people and accepts them with magnanimity, liberality, tolerance, and leniency. Second, the *kanyo* person does not blame, censure, find fault, or rebuke. Third, he or she acknowledges the right of others to declare minority, heretical opinions and takes no discriminatory treatment against such opinions. Fourth the Japanese do not persecute for past sins as in the very important Christian virtues. Not explicitly explained in detail, but fully connoted, is the virtue of not getting angry.

All thinking must be generously treated. Thinking must be treated as in an early learning state. They are incoate, as if the event never existed before. For persons in cultures who are educated in debating, argumentation, and quickly finding conclusions, the *kanyo* point of view will seem frustratingly inconclusive. It is a reality among the Japanese and, likely, in other cultures with Buddhist influences.

Clearly Hideo was a steadfast proponent of *kanyosei*, though he never explained his beliefs or behavior. By acquiring these sensibilities through experience and tacit understandings, many Nisei in US concentration camps and in military service of the United States demonstrated their strength of *kanyosei* with their quiet endurance, service, and valor. Uniformly, they purposely avoided talking about the injustices and enormous violations of rights. Many showed the strength of their belief, ultimately, with their lives. Former Pvt. Satoru Onodera was among the thousands of Nisei in the military service who said only by doing.

I will never forget Satoru's mother, whose sense of *kanyo* no doubt became part of Satoru's character. Our families were both incarcerated in concentration camp Minidoka. As a young teenager I worked as a messenger boy delivering Western Union telegrams throughout the barracks community. On one delivery, as I approached the door of Barrack 5 on that hot summer day, I did not know the contents of the telegram that was addressed to Mrs. Onodera, nor did I know that she had three sons in the army. But I knew it was not good, there could be no mistake.

"Oba-san. Good afternoon." I said. Her eyes brightened a bit. I felt as if I was talking to my mother. "This is a telegram." There was no avoiding my mission.

Before she read the telegram, Mrs. Onodera courteously asked me to come in for a while out of the sun and sit for a little while on the small porch of the tar paper barrack. The telegram I delivered on that hot summer day remained impersonal, but I knew in my soul that it was not good. As much as I tried, I was unable to shake that nagging feeling.

"Konnichi wa. Doko no boy dessho?" (Which family are you from?) she asked. If she knew English, she avoided its use and talked to me as a member of the extended family that we were in the camps. She held the telegram as if it were an ordinary item from her kitchen. Holding the telegram, Mrs. Onodera entered the barrack and reappeared with a glass of water for me. *"Atsui kara sukoshi yasumi nasai"* (It's so hot you had better rest awhile).

Out of respect for her kindness, I stayed, grateful for the cold water that quenched my thirst. Then I thanked her, got on my bike, and slowly pedaled away. I could see her on the porch with the telegram. I could see her like I saw too many mothers. The drabness of the barrack contrasted so sharply with her dignity. She looked at the envelope and walked inside.

I was among other messenger boys who became the bearer of momentous news in those years from 1943 to 1945. We carried envelopes with simple words to the parents of sons who were killed in action in Italy, France, Leyte, or some other battlefield in the Pacific. We were not accompanied by a uniformed officer to convey the sympathy of the War Department or the President. We were, as on that day when I carried the news of Satoru Onodera's death, alone. If the killed in action notices had been conveyed in a community on the outside, beyond the barbed wires, they would have been accompanied by a uniformed member of the US military with pomp and circumstance. The betrayal of citizenship and the outrage committed against civility defies description.

Just as Mrs. Onodera's behavior displayed her adherence to *kanyo*, Hideo's composure during his ordeal attests his discipline. He was sent back to Japan on the *Gripsholm*, which sailed through neutral waters, to Rio de Janeiro, Brazil, and around Cape of Good Hope to Mozambique. The exchange between the shipload of U.S. personnel from Japan and ethnic Japanese (for the most part) from the U.S. occurred at Lourenco Marques, Mozambique. The ship, *Asama Maru*, returning Hideo to Japan, arrived in Yokohama on August 20, 1942.

Hideo's daughter, Yoshiko Joy, said "I remember Dad walking down the pier toward Mom and me carrying his golf bag over his shoulder. I don't know where his golf bag was while he was in jail and the concentration camps, but the authorities gave it back to him when he boarded the ship. Mom wished he had left the bag in the U.S., because it was the most useless item to have in Japan at that time."

After nearly 40 years away, Hideo Okamoto returned to Japan. Unlike Rip Van Winkle, however, Hideo Okamoto was prepared for work in wartime Japan. He found employment at Mitsubishi Heavy Industries Shipbuilding Division, in Yokohama. He and his family lived in Meguro, Tokyo, so he commuted on the Toyoko Railroad Line. At Mitsubishi Zosen, American and British prisoners of war (POWs) were used as laborers at the plant. The American POWs lived in an adjacent camp under the severe discipline of the Japanese Army. Hideo, being fluent in English, became the primary liaison contact between the Mitsubishi Company, the Japanese military, and the POWs. He visited both plant and camp daily to make sure there were no problems or to deal with whatever situation that might be occurring. There were frequent problems because of the severity of military discipline and lack of adequate food.

Hideo became a good friend of U.S. Army Major Frank Grady who was the commanding officer of the prisoners at the camp. He was a particularly important prisoner, but the Japanese were unable to unearth the fact that he was one of America's key cryptanalysts. He was probably the man in charge of CAST, the code breaking unit in Corregidor in the Philippines. He was also the person in charge of the POW mess hall. The latter assignment was particularly important since all of Japan was on near starvation standards. Hideo often ate lunch with Frank in the POW kitchen, but Hideo's was a skimpy one prepared at home because of the lack of food on the open market. Although the Japanese military forces constantly guarded the prison camp, permitting no one to visit, Hideo could freely go in and out because of his position at Mitsubishi and his fluency in two languages. The military supplied food directly to the prisoners, so that the prisoners of war were, in reality, actually eating better than the Japanese civilian population. For an American, a Nisei who had the best of food in New York, including *sansai* delicacies, the Japanese diets in Tokyo and Yokohama were intolerable. At best, they caused quick malnutrition. Hideo's family was "hungry all the time." Frank could see from what Hideo had in his lunchbox that the POW food, occasionally fried fish, was considerably better than Japanese civilian food, even though the POWs themselves constantly complained about their food.

Whenever Hideo ate with Frank, a few times a week, Frank would slip POW food into Hideo's lunchbox to "take home to his daughter." Frank knew that Hideo had a daughter at home. In one of the grand ironies of the war and one that had to be kept secret from Japanese authorities, an American prisoner of war helped the Okamoto family with its nutritional needs in a "free," but starving, Japan.

Joy explained, "My father's work at Mitsubishi Heavy Industries during the late stages of World War II was important in its own way. I remember an incident at the POW camp, told to me at the time by my father, when the Japanese officers were outraged because they claimed some bread was stolen at the camp and they were determined to find the culprit and punish him."

Hideo was very sympathetic to the plight of the young men who were POWs. He used to say "they are kids, mostly under 20; war has no meaning for them; they have no idea why they have to be prisoners in Japan." If anything, Hideo thought war was a crime, and the young POWs were victims of that crime. Hideo wanted to help make their circumstances less miserable, if he could. Hideo told the Japanese officers to let him handle the situation by himself, and that he would try to find out who stole the bread. He had all the prisoners line up in rows at the far end of a muddy field and as he walked down the rows inspected each prisoner who took off his shirt. Down the second or third row when one man took off his shirt, bread crumbs fell out. Without saying a word, Hideo bent down and stuffed all the tiny pieces of bread together with the mud coating them into his mouth. As he kept walking down the rows, he gulped down his mouthful of crumbs and mud. He then walked to where the officers were and told them that hunting for a bread thief was futile.

A very tragic story involved a young American POW, about 18 or 19 years old, who accidentally fell off a high scaffolding at the Mitsubishi Shipyard and was critically injured. Hideo often visited him at the hospital and asked if he needed anything. The young man asked weakly, "Can you get me a banana?" He just wanted a bite of a banana. Unfortunately, there just were no bananas at Mitsubishi or the POW camp. In wartime Japan, no stores anywhere had any fresh food to offer. Hideo arrived home that evening and asked Fusako if she might be able to get a banana somewhere. Joy said, "It was a very difficult request; it was nearly as difficult as asking my mother to dig a hole in the backyard to find a large diamond."

In desperation, both Hideo and Fusako decided to go around the neighborhood asking each family if they just might have a banana to give, an absurd request from Joy's point of view. Besides, they could not dare tell anyone the banana was to give to an American prisoner of war. That would have been tantamount to treason. While they knew it would be an impossible search, more likely a miracle, they needed to try. Fortunately, they were very well-liked in the neighborhood, so neighbors were willing to help if they could. In an amazingly turn of events, Fusako arrived home, beaming, with a banana in hand! Joy was in disbelief; she had not seen one in ages. She was so surprised that she never asked which family had this literal treasure, a fresh banana.

Next morning, Hideo took the first train, at about 4:00 a.m., to Yokohama to take the banana to the dying prisoner in the hospital. Hideo reported to his family that when he took it to him; he smiled broadly and had one bite, looked content, and lost consciousness peacefully. He must have been waiting all night for a taste of that banana. Normally not emotional, Hideo wept unabashedly when he told his family about this young American POW. He had a special understanding of those young men who, by no fault of their own, were trapped in an untenable situation. Hideo had profound but seldom expressed sympathy and an identification with Americans. His tolerance, equanimity, and need for harmony remained the most important of all, subsuming the mistreatment given him by American law enforcement agencies as an enemy in their midst, the huge personal losses, and the incinerating bombing attacks on Tokyo and Yokohama in which he suffered permanent, crippling injuries.

Joy described what happened:

> In May, the air raids over Yokohama intensified. During one of them, Dad had gone to check on the POWs, had fallen in the industrial area, and injured his back. There was no medical care of any sort available at that time. The bombings knocked out the trains between Yokohama and Tokyo. From Meguro, we could see the red sky in the direction of Yokohama as we worried about what was happening to Dad. I think it was a couple of days later, as we waited looking down the road, wondering. The Toyoko Railroad Line was not running. I will always remember the sight of Dad, bent like an old, old man slowly trudging down the road toward our house. He had walked all the way from Yokohama, with the severe pain in an injured back. It must have been agonizing. We could not get medical attention for slipped discs in his back at that time. Understandably, he suffered for weeks, but he did recover enough to be able to function. In fact, he kept working continuously until his death in 1979. I do know that from the time the war ended right

until his death, he had a masseur come to the house nightly to massage his back. After the war, when he tried to get medical help, he was told the back had already healed itself.

On August 15, 1945, the war ended. Japan was defeated. Frank Grady became a Colonel and also served as a witness for the International War Crimes Tribunal, trying some of the Japanese officials who had mistreated the American prisoners of war.

Hideo was never put on trial. The American prisoners of war all signed a petition on his behalf.

In 1979, at the age of 87, Hideo Okamoto passed away. He survived War Plan Orange, governmental injustices, and prejudicial undercurrents which individuals of Japanese descent living in America had to encounter in the years of World War II. Though he himself was a victim of rampant racial discrimination and falsely arrested as a prisoner of war, he looked upon others without anger or blame. He lived the Issei life of *kanyo*—that humaneness must always be sought. That all is said by doing.

Supplementary Information

How to Find Documents in the National Archives

In simplified explanation, the National Archives are a public library. The scale of it makes it different. It is like a spread out town. Anyone can use the facilities and librarians are there to help the researcher. Formerly classified documents—those dealing with War Plan Orange were secret, there was no Top Secret classification in the early periods—can be hard to find. The difficulty arises from the fact that the researcher does not know where to look. I tried three times and only scratched the surface.

I found professional researchers who are there full time. Their services are cheap in my estimation, if the individual researcher calculates airfares, hotel bills, transportation, etc. The research firm I use is Nichimy Corporation in Tokyo.

Biographic Information on Hideo Okamoto

Nearly the entirety of the information about Hideo Okamoto comes from his daughter, Joy Tsuzuki, nee Okamoto. I have known Joy for fifty years; we worked together for a period in the early 1950s at the 6004th Air Intelligence Squadron in Tokyo. There were about forty Nisei working there. Joy and I have kept in touch and she provided information about her father via email.

I had met Hideo Okamoto a couple of times in Tokyo, but they were brief encounters. Of course, Hideo never complained of mistreatment by the US government.

Dictionary Definition of *Kanyo*

The *New Nelson Japanese English Character Dictionary*, based on the Classic Edition by Andrew N. Nelson, completely revised by John H. Haig and the Department of East Asian Languages and Literatures University of Hawaii at Manoa defines *kanyo* as "forbearance, tolerance, generosity." It's derivations—*kanyo no, kanyo shugi,* and *kanyo sei*—also describe those practicing *kanyo* as lenient, long-suffering, broad minded, liberal, and magnanimous.

Not explicitly stated in the dictionary: a characteristic of the Japanese.

Kanyosei is Common Knowledge in Japan

Anyone educated and brought up in Japan can explain *kanyo* to you. I encountered it in my English conversation classes in Imari. The adult members were quick to explain the term to me because of my ignorance of the Japanese cultural trait. As far as I know, US cultural anthropologists are unaware of the characteristic. It is an adjunct of Japanese endurance, *gaman suru.*

Appendix 1

Joint Army Navy Board No 355 paper authorizing American bombing raids against Japan

Several months before Japan's December 7, 1941 attack on Pearl Harbor, President Franklin Roosevelt secretly authorized devastating American bombing raids against Japanese cities. A top secret document de-classified in 1970, but only made public a few years ago, shows that in July 1941 Roosevelt and his top military advisers approved a daring plan to use American pilots and American war planes—deceitfully flying under the Chinese flag—to bomb Japan's major cities.

The bombers would be under the command of Claire Chennault, a former U.S. Air Corps flyer who had been in the employ of Chinese Generalissimo Chiang Kai-Shek since 1937. In July 1941, Chennault already headed the "American Volunteer Group" squadron of U.S. "Flying Tiger" fighter planes that fought with great success against Japanese forces in China. Chennault's colorful unit was glorified in American newspapers and magazines, and in the 1942 Hollywood propaganda motion picture Flying Tigers, starring John Wayne.

The young pilots who flew the distinctively "shark-toothed" B-40 warplanes were ostensibly mercenaries, and the AVG force had no official connection with the U.S. government. In reality, though, the squadron was secretly organized and funded by Washington—in flagrant violation of both American and international law. Set up without consultation or consent of Congress, it specifically violated the U.S. Neutrality Act, the Reserves Act of 1940, and the Selective Service Act of 1940. Chennault's squadron was also a breach of Roosevelt's own formal declarations of U.S. neutrality in the conflict between Japan and China, which had been raging since 1937.

By aiding China, Roosevelt sought to keep Japanese forces tied up there. As long as the Japanese were fully occupied in China, he thought, they would not be a threat to British and U.S. interests in Asia. If China fell, Britain would have to divert war ships, troops, and materiel badly needed in Europe.

A secret memorandum from the Office of the Chief of Naval Operations dated January 17, 1940 confirms that almost two years before the Pearl Harbor attack, the Roosevelt administration was considering war against the Japanese with U.S. mercenaries organized in "an efficient guerrilla corps." The memo also discussed a clandestine U.S. combat air operation against Japanese forces. Some months later, in May 1941, another memorandum for Roosevelt from Admiral Thomas C. Hart, Commander of the U.S. Asiatic fleet, began: "The concept of a war with Japan is believed to be sound," and went on to discuss how Japan could be attacked by American-piloted bombers. To put such ideas into effect, Chenault pushed for the formation of a task force of American-piloted bombers under his command that would raid Japan itself. "If the men and equipment were of good quality, such a force could cripple the Japanese war effort," he wrote. "A small number of long-range bombers carrying incendiary bombs could quickly reduce Japan's paper-and-matchwood cities to heaps of smoking ashes."

Chennault's proposal quickly received the enthusiastic support of China's ambassador in Washington, T. V. Soong (multi-millionaire banker brother-in-law of Chinese Generalissimo Chiang Kai-Shek), British ambassador Lord Lothian, U.S. Secretary of State Cordell Hull, and FDR's Treasury Secretary Henry Morgenthau.

The idea to bomb Japan was first formally presented to Roosevelt on December 19, 1940. As Dr. Duane Schultz relates in his 1987 study, The Maverick War, FDR's response was to exclaim "Wonderful!," and to immediately instruct his Secretaries of State, Treasury, War and Navy to begin working out the details of a battle plan. Not everyone was so enthusiastic, though. Secretary of War Henry Stimson and Army Chief of Staff General George Marshall expressed misgivings. Marshall cautioned that having American pilots bomb Japan using American planes with Chinese markings was a trick that would not really fool anybody, but would simply plunge the United States into a war with Japan at a time when the U.S. was still woefully unprepared.

As a result of such misgivings, the plan was temporarily shelved.

A few months later, though, a somewhat modified version was revived as "Joint Army-Navy Board Paper No. 355."

Roosevelt's order to attack Japan, July 23, 1941

The official U.S. "Joint Army-Navy Board No. 355" paper authorizes American bombing raids against Japan. The top secret document is signed by the Secretaries of War and Navy, and bears Franklin Roosevelt's initials of authorization and a handwritten date, July 23, 1941—more than four months before the Japanese attack against Pearl Harbor.

As finally laid out in JB 355, an air strike force of 500 Lockheed Hudson bombers was to be organized as "The Second American Volunteer Group" under Chennault's command. Its mission would be the "pre-emptive" bombing of Japan. The strategic objective of JB 355 was the "destruction of Japanese factories in order to cripple munitions and essential articles for maintenance of economic structure in Japan." From bases about 1,300 miles away in eastern China, the American bombers would strike Japan's industrial centers, including Osaka, Nagasaki, Yokohama and Tokyo. (These air strikes would have unavoidably claimed the lives of many civilians. By contrast, the Japanese planes that attacked Pearl Harbor carefully avoided civilian targets.)

U.S. funds for the operation were to be provided as part of a general loan to China and channeled through a dummy corporation. The American military personnel involved were given deceptive passports. (Chennault's gave his occupation as "farmer," and cited him as an "advisor to the Central Bank of China.) Secret plan JB 355 was approved by the Secretary of War, the Secretary of the Navy, and—on July 23, 1941—by President Franklin Roosevelt.

No one played a more important role in promoting and organizing this plan than Lauchlin Bernard Currie, a close Roosevelt White House adviser. Now 89 years old and living in South America, he provided details of his role in the secret operation, and of Roosevelt's support for it, in a November 1991 television interview. A major motive behind Currie's eagerness to get the U.S. into war with Japan, it seems, was his strongly pro-Soviet sympathies. There is even tantalizing but still inconclusive evidence to suggest that Currie was a Soviet agent. When Roosevelt approved plan JB 355, Currie sent a secret cable to Chennault: "I am very happy to be able to report that today the President directed that 66 bombers be made available to China this year, with 24 to be delivered immediately."

Although it received approval from numerous high-level officials, the plan was not well conceived. In the view of Yale University history professor Gaddis Smith, the Lockheed Hudson bombers that were to carry out the raids would have been easily shot down by Japan's first-rate fighter planes.

Two days after approving JB 355, Roosevelt declared a crippling trade embargo against Japan, an act of economic strangulation that he knew full well would virtually assure war. (At that time, about 90 percent of Japan's oil and iron came from the United States.) And having broken Japanese codes, British and American officials learned in early July of Japan's sure intentions in the Pacific: war with the U.S. was now inevitable.

Understandably viewing Roosevelt's campaign as a mortal threat to their country's very existence as a modern industrial nation, Japan's leaders resolved to strike a first blow. They reasoned that by destroying the U.S. Pacific fleet in Hawaii in one decisive surprise attack, they would remove the one great obstacle to forging a self-sufficient Japanese empire in eastern Asia. History thus intervened to thwart Roosevelt's plan to bomb Japan. Before JB 355 Japan could be put into effect, and before Japan felt the full impact of FDR's trade embargo, the Japanese attacked Pearl Harbor—and Roosevelt had the open war with Japan that he had anticipated. In effect, Japan beat America to the punch.

On December 11, 1941, four days after the Pearl Harbor debacle, all further action on the JB 355 plan was suspended, and the bomber pilots who had been recruited were quickly incorporated into the regular U.S. armed forces. Franklin Roosevelt branded December 7, 1941, as "a date which will live in Infamy." And although many millions of Americans still regard Japan's "sneak attack" as the ultimate act of international deceit and treachery, it was hardly unique.

Just about every major power has resorted to surprise attack at one time or another, according to a study by British army officer and historian Sir Frederick Maurice. Between 1700 and 1870, he calculated, France carried out 36 surprise attacks, Britain 30, Austria twelve, Russia seven, Prussia seven, and the United States at least five. In 1801, Britain's Lord Nelson destroyed Denmark's fleet in a surprise attack on Copenhagen. In May 1846, the U.S. Army invaded Mexican territory before Congress got around to declaring that a state of war existed with Mexico. Far from feeling ashamed about it, Americans later elected as President the commander who had led the expedition, Zachary Taylor. In June 1967, Israel carried out a surprise attack against Egypt, and was widely praised in the U.S. for its adroit skill in destroying almost the entire Egyptian air force while it was still on the ground.

The long-suppressed story of FDR's plan to bomb Japan certainly deserves to be better known. As sensational as it is, though, it is only one chapter of the larger—and still largely unknown—story of Roosevelt's extensive and illegal campaign to bring a supposedly neutral United States into the Second World War. Indeed, even before the outbreak of war in Europe in September 1939, Roosevelt was secretly doing everything in his power to incite conflict there.

In the months before the Pearl Harbor attack, the American president accelerated his illegal campaign. For example, after Axis forces launched the fateful June 22,1941, "Barbarossa" attack against Soviet Russia, he promptly began sending American aid to Stalin. On July 25, 1941, Roosevelt froze Japanese assets of $130 million in the United States, thus ending trade relations. He closed the American-run Panama Canal to Japanese shipping. In June and July 1941, he dispatched U.S. troops to occupy Greenland and Iceland. And by September–October 1941, U.S. warships were actively engaging German U-boats in the Atlantic, in flagrant violation of U.S. and international law.

From a larger historical perspective, the magnitude of Roosevelt's undercover military operations against Japan and Germany, at a time when the U.S. was ostensibly neutral, dwarfs other, much ballyhooed, clandestine U.S. military operations in later years, such as President Reagan's help to the Nicaraguan "Contra" fighters, or the infamous Iran-Contra operation.

Appendix 2

Tokyo Club Syndicate

A ONI Report on Japanese Tokyo Club Syndicate with Interlocking Affiliations December 24, 1941 declassified May 14, 1985

CONFIDENTIAL

COPIES DESTROYED JAN 16 1974

DECLASSIFIED BY 1678 RFP/AHR ON 5/14/85

NAVY DEPARTMENT Office of Naval Intelligence Washington, D.C. December 24, 1941

SUBJECT: JAPANESE TOKYO CLUB SYNDICATE, WITH INTERLOCKING AFFILIATIONS.

NOTE: Prepared by the Counter-Subversion Section, Office of Naval Intelligence, from information received from various sources.

INTRODUCTION

Custodial Detention

With the sudden outbreak of hostilities between Japan and the United States on December 7, 1941, a comprehensive program for the detention of enemy aliens was put into operation. Hundreds of known dangerous suspects were rounded up, official representatives of the Axis Powers were put under surveillance or taken into custody and Alien Enemy Hearing Boards were appointed to inquire into the activities and loyalty of the individuals concerned. Aided by their recommendations, the U.S. Attorney General will decide whether an alien should be released unconditionally, paroled, or interned for the duration of the war.

RECENT JAPANESE ACTIVITIES IN LATIN AMERICA

Although handicapped by the detention of many of its key individuals, the Japanese Intelligence Network in this hemisphere continues in operation. Recent reports have been received of suspicious movements of Japanese in various parts of Latin America, particularly in Mexico. On December 13th, one vessel of the Japanese fishing fleet, the ALERT, which was captured off Costa Rica by a Navy Air Patrol, was found to be carrying some 10,000 gallons of Diesel fuel oil. The ALERT, of American registry, is partly owned and manned by Japanese. **At the time of her capture, it is believed she was headed for a rendezvous with an enemy submarine or surface raider**.

From Mexico have come numerous rumors that approximately five thousand Japanese are congregating at some undetermined point in strategic Baja California. In this connection, one hundred of a Japanese population of six hundred in and around Ensenada, recently left the region in a ship which had been anchored off the coast. Moreover, during the night of December 10, 1941, all Japanese nationals living in Tijuana disappeared, apparently because of a report that the Mexican Government was recruiting Chinese for their armed forces. Those Japanese who remain are observed to be closely associated with Italians in the vicinity.

The Japanese practice of cloaking subversive operations with "legitimate business fronts" exists in Mexico as well as in the United States. Late in November, 1941, it was reported that Saburo YOSHITAKI, a button manufacturer of San Luis (near Mexicali) had installed short wave radio transmitting and receiving sets in his factory and that all of the Japanese in the surrounding district came there to listen. He is also believed to be connected with radio station KEY in Yuma, Arizona, and is considered potentially dangerous.

Strategically placed in Mexicali itself is one Yokoyama (or Chokichi) TAKAHASHI, a Japanese barber who, it is reliably reported, is a naval officer and also operates a short wave radio transmitter.

It also appears that the Japanese have placed Colonel Tadafumi WAKI, I.J.A., in an important position within their Intelligence Network in Mexico. Originally designated as the Assistant Military Attache of the Japanese Embassy in Washington, Colonel WAKI landed in Mexico on October 4, 1941, but there is no evidence that he ever came to this country. Reports believed to be reliable indicate that Colonel WAKI has in his possession maps of strategic areas in the Hawaiian Islands. Similar maps were reported to have been used by Japanese naval aviators in the attack on Pearl Harbor.

Japanese activities are by no means limited to Mexico. In Peru it is reported that the 30,000 or more Japanese living there are highly organized and that, following anti-Japanese riots, they distributed rifles to all their establishments. Here in the United States there has been reported a possible infiltration of Japanese espionage agents through Cuban and Florida ports. A similar danger exists with regard to the Pacific Coast and the Mexican border.

Since the outbreak of hostilities, Spanish Consuls in the U. S. have taken over all official business for the Japanese Consulates. Japanese collaboration with Spanish Fascist groups has also been extensively demonstrated in Mexico and the Philippine Islands. Among the organizations carrying on espionage and propaganda in the Philippines are LAS MISIONES JESUITE (JESUITICAS?) DEL JAPON, SOCIEDAD NIPO-ES ANCLA, FALANGE EXTERIOR ESPANOLA, and LIGA ANTI-COMINTERN ESPANOLA.

Isolated as these instances may appear to be, they are actually integral parts of a comprehensive hemispheric intelligence program which the Japanese have been developing for well over a year. The war has barely begun; undoubtedly before many more weeks elapse the significance of the Japanese planning will be more actively and clearly demonstrated.

Japanese Intelligence Machine in Western Hemisphere

Early in December, 1940, it became apparent that the Japanese were about to effect a comprehensive reorganization of their Intelligence Network in this hemisphere. At that time, soon after the arrival of Admiral Kichisaburo NOMURA as Ambassador, it was reported that the Japanese Government would intensify the espionage activities of their non-political agencies in this country, relaxing their former policy of "cultural enlightenment and propaganda."

In streamlining their Intelligence Machine the Japanese have been guided by two major considerations. In the first place, the totalitarian doctrines adopted by the Japanese military clique required as a corollary, some such system of "total intelligence" as the Germans have developed in recent years. This meant that the scope of propaganda, espionage, and sabotage activities and, in turn, the individuals and agencies responsible for that coverage had to be enlarged to include commercial, financial, industrial, and social spheres of action in addition to regular military, naval, and political operations.

Allied with this first consideration was the conviction, apparently shared by most members of the Japanese ruling clique, that Japan must act quickly to establish in the U.S. and Latin America a completely integrated intelligence organization which in time of war and the breaking off of official relations would be capable of taking over intelligence operations on a major scale.

Evidence of concrete steps taken to put this new Intelligence Machine into operation is available in numerous reports received during the spring of 1941. **From these it appears that the focal point of the Japanese espionage effort has been the determination of the total strength of the United States.** In anticipation of possible open conflict with this country, Japan vigorously utilized every available agency to secure military, naval, and commercial information, paying particular attention to the West Coast, the Panama Canal, and the Territory of Hawaii. To this end, surveys were made of persons and organizations opposing U.S. intervention in the present European War, and close attention was paid to all anti-Jewish, Communist, Negro, and Labor Movements.

Although never fully developed, this new espionage organization was characterized by a high degree of decentralization. Before the outbreak of hostilities the activity of the military and naval section, which was divided into a number of different groups, was supplemented by the work of independent agents, and the general pattern included individuals, small groups, and commercial organizations functioning separately and energetically. In the background lay the Imperial Japanese Government, which until recently exercised direct control over both individuals and organizations through the Embassy and the Consulates.

The new program provided for the utilization of citizens of foreign extraction, aliens, Communists, Negroes, Labor union members, anti-Semites, and individuals having access to Government Departments, experimental laboratories, factories, transportation facilities, and governmental organizations of various kinds. Nisei (second generation) Japanese and alien Japanese residents were not overlooked. Realizing, however, that its nationals in this country would be subject to prosecution "in event of a slip," the Japanese Government advised extreme caution in their employment.

It was also decided that, in the event of open hostilities, Mexico would be Japanese intelligence nerve center in the Western Hemisphere, and in anticipation of war, U.S.-Latin American intelligence routes were established. This network, covering Argentina, Brazil, Chile, Peru, and the Central American countries, is designed to operate from Mexico City and will, of necessity, involve extensive cooperation among Japanese, German, and Italian intelligence organizations.

Outstanding among the espionage projects of the Japanese Army and Navy were their comprehensive and systematic surveys of the entire western coast of North America. Similar studies have been made of the inland western mountain area. The total body of information covers every conceivable military objective—railroads, highways, rivers, key industries, terrain features, etc. Needless to state, military and naval installations also received close attention.

Japanese propaganda in the U.S, has for the most part been under the direction of a special division of the Japanese Foreign Office in Tokyo. Local control was administered through the Embassy in Washington, D.C., as well as through the Consulates in key cities and Consular Agents in regions having Japanese communities. The media employed ranged from radio broadcasts and printed matter to subsidized speakers and underworld "pressure" groups. Private business firms, as well as official and quasi-official agencies, have been particularly active in propaganda dissemination. At the same time they rendered invaluable service to the Japanese Army and Navy in the acquisition of technical information.

The Tokyo Club Syndicate

It is believed that the organizations treated in this present report offer an excellent illustration of the extremely complicated interlockings which frequently characterize Japanese groups. What would appear to be legitimate businesses and totally unrelated activities are shown to have a definite community of interests as well as administrative and financial connections. **These inter-relationships are far too numerous to be termed coincidental and are at the same time of a definitely subversive nature.**

The TOKYO CLUB of Los Angeles, with its chief subsidiaries, the NICHIBEI KOGYO KAISHA (NICHIBEI KINEMA CO.) of Los Angeles and the TOYO CLUB of Seattle, until very recently constituted the nucleus of a system of gambling clubs extending from Alaska to Tijuana and Mexicali, Mexico. Through extensive use of interlocking directorates and high-pressure methods, the sphere of control was gradually extended to numerous other individuals and organizations. Concomitantly there were developed or imposed elements of control by the Japanese Consulates and Japanese Army and Navy officials on the West Coast. The result has been to convert a widespread decentralized system of Japanese "clubs," labor organizations, and legitimate business groups **into an important unit of the central Japanese Intelligence Network**.

The organizations involved number six and are **suspected of such diverse activities as dope smuggling, espionage, extortion, fishing, gambling, labor organization and control, murder, police bribery, propaganda, radio, and the operation of business "fronts," canneries, courier routes, and "post offices."** Many of the individuals involved are classed as dangerous suspects and have interlocking affiliations among both these and other subversive organizations. There can be no doubt that most of the leaders have been and that many still continue to function as key operatives for the Japanese Government along the West Coast. Under present wartime conditions both they and their subordinates constitute a very serious threat to our internal security in the areas where they operate.

Case Histories and Schematic Diagrams

The attached case histories and diagrams provide essential detailed information with respect to both the individual organizations and their interlocking affiliations. The tabulation showing the leaders with their various activities (designated by "x" under the vertical headings) is based upon an analysis of **various sources of information covering the period 1936–1941.** Each mark may be interpreted as representing an affiliation of definite and durable nature; in those cases where the connection was spasmodic, of brief duration, or in any way uncertain, a question mark has been added alongside the "x".

The diagram on the TOKYO CLUB NETWORK is designed to portray the geographical distribution as well as the diversity of function of the original TOKYO CLUB system. (Although a confidential report, dated 11/5/41, alleges that the TOKYO CLUB (sometimes called the LITTLE TOKYO SOCIAL CLUB) is no longer in existence, it is known that the TOYO CLUB has become the new headquarters.) The Los Angeles headquarters is shown in relationship to its subsidiaries in Alaska, Canada, and along the West Coast, as well as to other organizations with which it is affiliated through interlocking of officials or identity of interests.

The diagram also indicates the flow of information and control through Mexico and thence to Japan and Latin America. In this connection there should be kept in mind the proximity of San Diego to Tijuana and of El Centro to Mexicali, all four places, along with Yuma, Nogales, El Paso, Laredo, and Brownsville, being well known Japanese "post offices" and local espionage centers. With the advent of hostilities it seems safe to anticipate further development and utilization of these U.S.-Latin American intelligence channels.

TOKYO CLUB

(Formerly at 317 Jackson St.)
Los Angeles, California

OFFICERS: Present officers unknown.

SUMMARY:

BACKGROUND: The TOKYO (or TOKIO) Club was first organized about 1919 by one Jitetsu YASUDA as the center of a Pacific Coast gambling syndicate. The central club, it is reported, used thugs and gunmen to "shake down" the individual clubs, but at the same time offered them no protection or other services other than financial loans. During the ensuing years of the syndicate's operation there was a succession of leaders or bosses of the TOKYO CLUB; if a boss were not killed off beforehand, he would voluntarily return to Japan at the expiration of a customary 2–3 year term. It is also reported that bosses of the CLUB were schooled for their jobs by first serving as president of the affiliated NICHIBEI KOGYO KAISHA (see case history).

KANEKICHI YAMAMOTO CASE (1937–1938): YAMAMOTO, head of the Seattle TOYO CLUB, was deported January 23, 1939, from Seattle after having spent approximately one year in the Federal (McNeil Island) Penitentiary on an income tax fraud conviction. It appears from investigation reports on the case that YAMAMOTO's guilt was suggested to Government officials by one Hideichi YAMATODA, 1937 head of the TOKYO CLUB whose position was being threatened by YAMAMOTO. Tasaburo WAKATAKE, who had preceded YAMATODA as TOKYO CLUB president and who favored YAMAMOTO to succeed to the leadership of the syndicate, returned to Japan in February 1937; thus, when YAMAMOTO, too, was removed from the scene by his above-mentioned conviction, YAMATODA was left free to engineer a coup and assume full control of the club chain.

It was reported (March, 1938) that YAMAMOTO, for the sake of the future of the organization, had initiated efforts to patch up relations between the syndicate members, the TOKYO CLUB, and NICHIBEI KOGYO KAISHA. E. MORII of Vancouver, B.C., and S. YASUMURA of San Francisco acted as mediators, apparently motivated by the fear of what YAMAMOTO might report "to his principals in Japan."

YAMATODA KIDNAPING CONSPIRACY CASE (1938–): Having once gained the upper hand in the TOKYO CLUB and its affiliates, Hideyoshi YAMATODA was unable to maintain the strong and widespread organization which his predecessors had ruled through the use of gangster methods. Accordingly the syndicate broke down into separate clubs, the TOKYO CLUB remaining largest and most powerful and still controlling those clubs located at El Centro, Guadalupe, Visalia, Lodi, and elsewhere. In addition YAMATODA separated the JAPANESE THEATRICAL ASSOCIATION AND FILM EXCHANGE from the activities of the TOKYO CLUB. Since 1938 YAMATODA has posed as a film executive, using the NICHIBEI KOGYO KAISHA as his headquarters and front.

In the Fall of 1938 a group of New York Japanese gamblers, headed by one Kamenosuke YUGE, united with a group of West Coast Japanese gamblers, led by Mitsui TAGAWA, and formed a conspiracy to oust YAMATODA, seize control of the TOKYO CLUB and the JAPANESE THEATRICAL ASSOCIATION AND FILM EXCHANGE, and apparently, to rebuild the original TOKYO CLUB and unite it with the New York gambling hook-up. They obtained the assistance of certain Los Angeles police officers and in September 1938, managed to have YAMATODA arrested. YAMATODA later asserted that the police thereupon ordered him to leave Los Angeles and return to Japan within three months.

In the meantime YUGE and his associates had united with one Richard YOSHIDA and taken over the Japanese gambling club at El Centro, California, ousting Ryotaro IWAHASHI, who had operated the club some 10 years "as a lieutenant of the TOKYO CLUB." They also obtained the aid of the El Centro police chief, one J. Sterling OSWALT, in making the attempt to reconstruct the original gambling syndicate.

In December 1938, there occurred a kidnapping from the El Centro jail in which YAMATODA was the victim and YUGE, YOSHIDA, OSWALT, and others the kidnapers. Taken eventually to Mexico, YAMATODA escaped, gathered his friends to his aid, and returned to Los Angeles to press charges against the kidnapers. As a result of this charge, YUGE, OSWALT, and eight others were indicted by the Los Angeles Federal Grand Jury (9/6/39). The trial was never completed, owing to YAMATODA's flight to Japan in April, 1941, to avoid his prosecution for murder, which was scheduled to follow, but did result in YUGE, among others, being convicted of conspiracy and confined to McNeil Island Penitentiary.

CONCLUSION: The present status of the TOKYO CLUB in Los Angeles and its affiliated clubs and activities along the West Coast of the United States and in Alaska, British Columbia, Mexico, China, and Japan, is undetermined. However, in view of the extremely widespread and diversified nature of its operations in the past few years and, more particularly in the light of recently intensified Japanese espionage activities, it is deemed advisable to maintain a strict watch on the chief individuals formerly identified with subject club (inasmuch as they may resort to new "fronts" for their operations) and to investigate further their numerous interlocked connections with such subversive activities as canneries, fishing, espionage, propaganda, sabotage, etc.

(See schematic diagram, copy attached.)

FORMER PERSONNEL AND MEMBERS:

COUGHLIN, Ray T.—Sacramento (Calif.) attorney (White American) who reportedly managed the legal aspects of the establishment of the TOKYO CLUB syndicate.

FURUSAWA, (Mrs.) Koko—Class "A" suspect, wife of Dr. Takashi FURUSAWA who is likewise an "A" suspect. She is reported to have formerly been the wife of a Japanese naval officer (in Japan), whom she left to become a maid in a Japanese inn. Subsequently she came to the U. S. to work as a waitress in the Lil' Tokyo section of Los Angeles, and while there helped Takashi FURUSAWA through college, marrying him when he became established.

"Street scene in 'Little Tokyo' near the Los Angeles Civic Center." (04/11/1942)

To date Mrs. FURUSAWA is the only woman member of the extremely suspect SAKURA KAI [Cherry Association], and, with her husband, was a member of the group who founded the equally suspect KAIGUN KYOKAI [Navy League]. She holds office in the AIKOKU FUJIN KAI [Women's Patriotic Society] in California, a popular society for women, and is also a director of the SOUTHERN CALIFORNIA ASSOCIATION OF JAPANESE WOMEN'S CLUBS. Her widespread activities among Japanese naval and army officers warrant her being classified as an espionage and "post office" suspect.

HIRAO, Kana—Class "B" suspect, in frequent communication with Kanekichi YAMAMOTO and associated with him in the gambling syndicate from 1926 to 1938; thenceforth (after YAMAMOTO's deportation) until 1940, he continued his affiliation in the TOKYO CLUB. Was tried and convicted for illegal shipment of arms to Shanghai in 1939–1940.

ICHIKAWA, Hakui—Class "A" suspect, chief lieutenant of Kanekichi YAMAMOTO at the TOYO CLUB in Seattle prior to the latter's deportation in 1938. In 1937 he became active head of the club. Did much traveling and had repeated contacts with suspects "George" Naokazu ISHIBASHI, Dr. Benjamin Masayoshi TANAKA, OHTA, Takeyaki SASAKI, and consular and military-naval representatives.

Some time later he became proprietor of the STAR POOL HALL (517 Jackson Street, Seattle), reputed to be another gambling place. Is believed to have been behind the gun smuggling attempt of Kane HIRAO, and in turn probably had YAMAMOTO behind him at the time.

Most recent reports on ICHIKAWA (9/5/41 and 10/22/41) indicate that he has been extremely outspoken in his criticism of the appeasement efforts of certain Japanese statesmen which have prevented Japan's southward expansion. These same reports suggest that he hoped to return to Japan in the near future, that he had sold his pool parlor and had sent considerable sums to a former TOYO CLUB leader (probably Takeyaki SASAKI) at the KUMAMOTOYA HOTEL, Yokohama.

MARUYAMA, Norio—Nothing is known other than the fact that he was one of the officers who assumed control of the TOKYO CLUB syndicate when Hideyoshi YAMATODA took over its management in 1937.

MATSUMOTO, Ken (or Tai)—A lieutenant of Kanekichi YAMAMOTO in the TOYO CLUB and interested with him in the fishing-cannery business and labor contracting. May possibly be the Ken MATSUMOTO who is presently national vice president of the J.A.C.L.

MORI, Yatsuma—Closely affiliated with Kanekichi YAMAMOTO and the TOKYO CLUB chain through his position (1936) as official of the Los Angeles TOKYO CLUB, manager of LITTLE TOKYO CLUB, and director of the NICHIBEI KOGYO KAISHA (see case history of the latter).

MORII, Eitsuji—Alien, Class "A" suspect. Head of the JAPANESE CANADIAN AMUSEMENT SOCIETY, a part of the TOKYO CLUB syndicate, and reputedly leader of the Japanese in Vancouver. He was for a long time associated with Kanekichi YAMAMOTO in the TOKYO CLUB and NICHIBEI KOGYO KAISHA, does extensive traveling, and is classified as an espionage suspect.

OHTA, — —Early in 1939 he was reported to control Japanese gambling in Imperial Valley, California, and to be endeavoring to re-open the TOKYO CLUB in Los Angeles. (OHTA was supposed to have "fixed" the police to such an extent that he had complete control of Japanese gambling throughout Southern California.)

SMALLPAGE, Lafayette—Stockton (California) attorney (White American) who participated in the organization of the TOKYO CLUB as legal adviser.

SUZUKI, Makoto—Class "B" suspect who has posed as a member of the Japanese fishing colony at Terminal Island. He is suspected of being a Japanese agent and of having recently traveled in South America.

TOMINAGA, Keisuke—Aide to Hideyoshi YAMATODA in the TOKYO CLUB (1937–) and also a contact of Kanekichi YAMAMOTO (1936). Was for some time suspected of participation in a dope smuggling ring as "delivery man" for the CLUB.

WAKATAKE, Tasaburo—Nothing known other than his early leadership in subject syndicate. Is believed to have returned to Japan.

YAMAMOTO, Kanekichi (or Kinpachi)—Head of the Seattle TOYO CLUB and one of the heads of the NICHIBEI KOGYO KAISHA (see case history) who was slated to assume leadership of the TOKYO CLUB system, under the sponsorship of WAKATAKE, as stated above in the summary. This plan was thwarted by the income tax case which resulted in YAMAMOTO's imprisonment and subsequent deportation in 1939. He was also interested in the fishing-cannery business and the organization of related labor unions (see case histories on the ALASKA CANNERY WORKERS UNION and the CANNERY WORKERS AND FARM LABORERS UNION). At present he is reported to be in Shanghai, probably active in the Chinese-Manchurian clubs of subject organization for which SASAKI used to be the contact.

YAMATODA, Hideyoshi (or Hideichi)—Class "A" suspect and for some time (1938–1941) the "boss" of the TOKYO CLUB syndicate and the closely affiliated NICHIBEI KOGYO KAISHA (see case history). In addition he was a member of the dangerous SAKURA KAI and maintained intimate contacts among Japanese consular and military-naval officials. It should also be noted that the TOKYO CLUB's murder trade was quite brisk during the period of YAMATODA's leadership; he himself is suspected of having committed some of the crimes (see Summary above).

Following his kidnapping and the unfinished trial which resulted from it, YAMATODA fled to Japan via Mexico and is presently being sought there by the U. S. Department of State.

YASUMURA, S.—Nothing is known save his membership in subject club.

(For further information on above individuals see schematic diagram and supplement on TOYO CLUB.)

TOKYO CLUB—Supplement

TOYO CLUB

SUMMARY:

The club which ranked second, next in importance to the TOKYO CLUB in Los Angeles, was the TOYO CLUB of Seattle. While posing as a gambling establishment, as have the parent and other sister organizations, this club actually carried on such "extra-curricula" activities as dope smuggling, police "fixing," espionage, cooperation with labor unions in fishing-cannery interests, etc.

It is reliably reported that subject club was established by a Japanese named SASAKI (probably Takeyaki, alias Tosayama, SASAKI, see pp. 3, 5 of this report), who returned to Japan a number of years ago to become the gambling syndicate's representative there as well as in North China and Manchoukuo. After SASAKI's departure the club was operated by Kanekichi YAMAMOTO, who employed Seiichi "Sam" TAKENO (since deceased), Hakui ICHIKAWA (see p. 3), and one J. NAKATSU—all of whom are suspects—to assist him. When YAMAMOTO left the U. S.

in 1939, after serving his prison term, his three assistants inherited the club and its business, ICHIKAWA eventually becoming the most active of the group. Shoichi NOJIMA, son-in-law of NAKATSU and a Class "A" suspect, does the bookkeeping for the club.

In connection with TAKENO, who died August 17, 1941, it should be noted that he resided with a Japanese woman known as Mrs. S. FURUMOTO and, with her, operated the NEW CENTRAL CAFE of Seattle.

Listed under Personnel are names of a few of the Japanese who were at one time or another in recent years, identified with the TOYO CLUB. ONI also has in its possession a comprehensive list of the contacts of Kanekichi YAMAMOTO, acquired at the time of his arrest in 1937. Many of them are Class "A" suspects.

PERSONNEL:

ASAKURA, Makutaro—Class "A" suspect, proprietor of the STACY STREET TAVERN (see appended list of Restaurants, Cafes, etc.). Entered the United States illegally but have been here too long for deportation. Was at one time connected with the TOYO CLUB as dealer both at the club and in logging camps.

FUKAO, "Paul" Kenichi—Class "A" suspect and a henchman of Kanekichi YAMAMOTO. In January, 1941, was reported to be employed by the TOYO CLUB as lottery ticket salesman and driver of the car operated by the club to transport Japanese crews back and forth between ship and club.

HASHIMOTO, "Hashi"—Class "A" suspect.

IMAIZUME, Yasugi—Class "A" suspect.

KANAGAWA, Sho (Tadashi or Masa).

KOMATSU, Ryo (Riyo)—Class "A" suspect.

KONO, Junsaku—Class "A" suspect and special henchman of Hakui ICHIKAWA. In February 1941, was reported to be employed as a dealer at the gambling tables of the STAR POOL HALL (owned by ICHIKAWA).

MORIMIZU, "Tony" Rinta—Japanese citizen, Class "A" suspect. Was, in January, 1941, president of the PUGET SOUND VEGETABLE

GROWERS ASSOCIATION and considered to be one of the three most influential Japanese in the White River Valley area. In 1938, 1939, and 1941 was president of the JAPANESE ASSOCIATION of Sumner, Washington. Was also active in the KUMAMOTO PREFECTURAL ASSOCIATION in 1939 and 1940.

NAGAMATSU, Henry Heiji—(See case history on JAPANESE CANNERIES).

NAKATSU, Jiutaro (alias Jintaro, Gintaro, etc.)—Class "A" suspect. Subject was active in the 1937 Sumo Tournament at Seattle and for some time gunman for the TOYO CLUB and private bodyguard to YAMADA (once head of said club). In March 1941, was still a leader in sumo groups and an adviser of the KUMAMOTO OVERSEAS ASSOCIATION. It is believed his son-in-law has returned to Japan, but NAKATSU continues to participate in the management of the TOYO CLUB.

OBATA, K.—Class "A" suspect and operator of a restaurant located at 604 Main Street, Seattle (probably the ROSE CAFE). During fishing-canning season OBATA had worked as foreman at an Alaskan Cannery. It should also be noted that it was at his residence that Kanekichi YAMAMOTO went into hiding from U.S. Treasury authorities in 1937.

OGAMI, Teiichi—Japanese citizen, Class "A" suspect. He is proprietor of the OGAMI SACK CO., which handles second hand gunnysacks and is located at 809 Maynard Avenue, Seattle. As early as 1935 and 1936, OGAMI was known to be an intimate of Kanekichi YAMAMOTO and of other Japanese suspects, Sataro MINAMI (deceased) among them. He has also been active in Japanese activities in the Seattle region. In 1938 he was one of the vice presidents of the suspect HOKUBEI BUTOKU KAI [Military Virtue Society of North America]. In 1939 he was treasurer and in 1940 vice president of the OKAYAMA PREFECTURAL ASSOCIATION. Was also one of the Japanese who were honored with a wooden sake cup by the Japanese Foreign Office on the occasion of the 2600th Anniversary Celebration held in Tokyo in November, 1940.

This past year he has been reported as having donated money to the SEATTLE JAPANESE CHAMBER OF COMMERCE, the HOKUBEI BUTOKU KAI, the BUDDHIST CHURCH, and to a local kendo club.

The U. S. Immigration Service reports that he entered the United

States in 1921. Business associates state that he is of good reputation and not outspokenly pro-Japanese.

SAITO, (Dr.) Moriya—Class "A" suspect and a dentist with office at 670 Jackson Street, Seattle. In February, 1941, he was reported to operated gambling tables at the NIPPON POOL HALL on Main Street, Seattle (see appended list of Restaurants, Cafes, etc.) and to have been intimate with Kanekichi YAMAMOTO.

Subject may possibly be the "Hori SATO" of Seattle who is listed as a member of the suspect HINOMARU KAI [Round Sun (flag) Association; similar to usage of "Stars and Stripes" to describe the US flag].

SAKAINO, Bunro (Fumiro)—Class "A" suspect, editor of "THE COAST TIMES" a newspaper of Portland, and secretary in 1940 of both the JAPANESE ASSOCIATION of Portland and the suspect SOKOKU KAI [Ancestral Country Society]. Is an intimate of "George" Haoichi ISHIBASHI (see case history on JAPANESE CANNERIES) as well as of Hakui ICHIKAWA (see above). SAKAINO was one of 17 Japanese residents in 13 ND who were honored with wooden sake cups by the Japanese Foreign Office on the occasion of the 2600th Anniversary Celebration held in Tokyo in November, 1940.

SAKAMOTO, Tamizo—(See case history on JAPANESE CANNERIES).

SUYETANI, "Roy" Kiyoshi—**Class "A" suspect**, listed in the Seattle City Directory as a chauffeur. Was, for some time, bodyguard and gunman for Kanekichi YAMAMOTO and other leaders of the TOYO CLUB. His wife (?) is connected with the NIPPON POOL HALL referred to above, and he himself is presently reported to be head of subject club and "fixer" for the local Japanese community.

TATEOKA (TAKEOKA), Hisashi—**Class "A" suspect.**

NICHIBEI KOGYO KAISHA (Japanese-American Theatrical Company)

NICHIBEI KINEMA., INC.
NICHIBEI KINEMA KAISHA
GREAT FUJI (FUJII) THEATER

HEADQUARTERS: Yokohama, Japan

U.S. Main Branch: 201 N. San Pedro Street, Los Angeles, California

OFFICERS:

KUMAMOTO, Shunten (Shinsuke)	-	President
NARUMI, Jutaro	-	Vice President
HASUIKE, George Susumu	-	Vice President
UYEDA, Yaozo	-	Treasurer
KIDA, Masataro	-	Treasurer
TSUDA, Noboru	-	Director
KIMURA, Muneo	-	Managing Director
MUKAEDA, Katsuma	-	Auditor
BAN, Takeshi (Rev., Dr.)	-	Auditor

SUMMARY:

Subject company was first incorporated in December, 1937, and was originally controlled as a front for the LITTLE TOKYO GAMBLING CLUB, owned by Hideichi YAMATODA. After the latter's kidnapping in 1937, however, the leader of the Japanese community advised him that they believed the operation of subject company was a matter of vital interest to the community, and through pressure brought upon him, his interest in the company was reduced to two shares of a total of fifty. The remaining shares are held chiefly by officers in the CENTRAL JAPAN ASSOCIATION and the LOS ANGELES JAPANESE CHAMBER OF COMMERCE.

Articles of incorporation, dated April 22, 1939, show the purpose of the company to be buying and selling, and importing and exporting of still and motion pictures, films, and musical records; the contracting of players and actors; the booking of lectures, plays, and musical acts at theatrical places.

This organization has been distributing highly nationalistic Japanese films which portray Japanese expansion in Asia and the might of the Japanese Army. It is also believed to have booked lectures which praised Japanese customs as being superior to American.

On March 30, 1940, capitalization was increased from $25,000 to $250,000. Subject organization was reorganized March 5, 1941, and its names changed to NICHIBEI KINEMA COMPANY, INC. It is also known under the title JAPANESE THEATRICAL ASSOCIATION, INC., this being the name to which newsreels are consigned by the Yokohama headquarters.

PERSONNEL:

BAN, (Rev., Dr.) Takeshi—Japanese citizen, Class "A" suspect. In 1938 was reported to be a Doctor of Divinity, head of the JAPANESE SOCIETY OF RELIGIOUS EDUCATION, and minister of the CONGREGATIONAL CHURCH. A news articles in a Los Angeles Japanese paper (September, 1938) described BAN as having been an Imperial Army Officer during the Russo-Japanese War and as having won the Seventh Order of the Rising Sun for outstanding conduct. **At about the same time (i.e. September, 1938) he reportedly joined the suspect HOKUBEI HEIEKI GIMUSHA KAI. For the past several years he has been active in the leadership of the TAIHEIYO BUNKA KYOIKU KAI (Pacific Cultural Education Society) and at present is reported to be president of this organization. Recent information also shows him to hold office in the suspect NANKA TEIKOKU GUNYU-DAN.**

Since 1937 and up to the present time subject has been exceedingly active as a propagandist. He has lectured and has directed the distribution of nationalistic motion picture films along the West Coast and inland as far as Colorado. (In 1939, it was reported that he received subsidies from the JAPANESE TRADE PROMOTION BUREAU of the Ministry of Commerce for his propaganda activities.) In this connection it might be noted that the automobile which he used for his travels in 1938 carried, in addition to films and projector, all the necessary equipment for taking and developing motion pictures.

Because of the nature of his activities and the wide area over which he operates he is classified by ONI as an espionage suspect.

HASUIKE, Susumu—Citizenship unknown. Class "A" suspect. In 1940 subject was reported to be owner of the THREE STAR PRODUCE

COMPANY (932 Wall Street, Los Angeles, Calif.), also to be a member of the suspect SAKURA KAI, and to have donated $1,000 to the equally suspect NIPPON KAIGUN KYOKAI. In addition he has been very prominent in Japanese circles in Los Angeles and holds, or has held, office in several Japanese organizations other than those mentioned above.

KIDA, Masataro—A native of Shizuoka Prefecture, and probably a Japanese citizen, Class "B" suspect, occupation restaurant owner. In addition to his affiliation with the NICHIBEI KOGYO KAISHA, in which he is also a stockholder, KIDA is president of one of the Los Angeles Buddhist kendo organizations.

KIMURA, Muneo—Native of Yamaguchi Prefecture and probably a Japanese citizen, Class "B" suspect. As business manager of the NICHIBEI KOGYO KAISHA, KIMURA has made frequent "business trips" to the Hawaiian Islands and was one of the group of Japanese, lead by Shunten KUMAMOTO, who went to Japan in 1940, ostensibly to engage a theatrical troupe for a U. S. tour. This troupe arrived in San Francisco on November 13, 1940, traveled extensively, and reportedly made numerous contacts for espionage purposes.

KIMURA has been reported as a member of both the SAKURA KAI and the NIPPON KAIGUN KYOKAI, but his affiliation with these organizations has not yet been confirmed.

KUMAMOTO, Shunten (Shinsuke)—Citizenship unknown, **Class "A" suspect.** During the past three years has been exceedingly active in Japanese organizations in the Los Angeles area. He is known to be auditor and director of the CULTURAL CENTER OF SOUTHERN CALIFORNIA and is also connected with the Los Angeles branch of the JAPAN TOURIST BUREAU, both of which organizations are Japanese propaganda agencies. Is an ex-president of the CENTRAL JAPANESE ASSOCIATION at Los Angeles, as well as of the LOS ANGELES JAPANESE CHAMBER OF COMMERCE, and has for some time been influential in the suspect SAKURA KAI.

His business concern, known as the S. K. PRODUCE CO., is reportedly backed by Keisuke TOMINAGA and the TOKYO CLUB (see case history on TOKYO CLUB).

In the latter part of 1940, KUMAMOTO visited Japan with

Muneo KIMURA for the purpose of **organizing a theatrical troupe (allegedly espionage agents)** and also to participate in the 2600th Anniversary Celebration. It is believed that at this latter convention he represented the CENTRAL JAPANESE ASSOCIATION, and, furthermore, that during the six months he was abroad he made an extensive study of conditions in various sections of Japan. Reports on the convention in Tokyo indicates that KUMAMOTO had entré to the Japanese Foreign Office, probably as member of its "non-official" staff, and that he participated in round table discussions sponsored by the Ministries of Foreign Affairs and Overseas Affairs.

MUKAEDA, Katsuma—Native of Kumamoto Prefecture, **Class "A" suspect**. He is a prominent attorney-at-law and pro-Japanese propagandist who has, in the past, been closely associated with the Japanese Consulate in Los Angeles. For the past eight years he has been active in Japanese nationalistic organizations and has, at the same time, been in contact with Japanese Navy and Army Officers.

In reward for his services to the Japanese Empire he was recently decorated by the Emperor and honored with a letter of commendation from the Foreign Office.

In 1933 MUKAEDA served as president of the FEDERAL JAPANESE ASSOCIATIONS OF SOUTHERN CALIFORNIA; in 1935 was president of the CENTRAL JAPANESE ASSOCIATION and a member of the organizing committee of the SOCIETY FOR ORIENTAL STUDIES of Claremont, California; in 1939 he was identified with both the SAKURA KAI and the JAPANESE CULTURAL CENTER OF SOUTHERN CALIFORNIA. It is also known that for some years past he has been contact man on the Pacific Coast for the JAPAN INSTITUTE (formerly of New York City), and that he is also a supporting member of the NIPPON KAIGUN KYOKAI. When the Japanese spy Lt. Cmdr. Itaru TACHIBANA, IJN [Imperial Japanese Navy], was arrested by the FBI in the Spring of 1941, MUKAEDA's name was mentioned in the material seized.

While president of the CENTRAL JAPANESE ASSOCIATION, subject established a new department with the name "JOHO-BU" (Intelligence Bureau), the main activities of which were to procure speakers to lecture on Japanese culture and, with the cooperation of the Los Angeles, and the KOKUSAI BUNKA SHINKO KAI (Society for the Promotion of International Cultural Relations) in Tokyo, to invite prominent Japanese lecturers to this country. Professor Ken NAKAZAWA, of the University of Southern California, assisted in this project.

Within the last several **months it has become apparent that MUKAEDA has been cooperating with the CENTRAL JAPANESE ASSOCIATION of Los Angeles in attempting to gain control of the JAPANESE AMERICAN CITIZENS LEAGUE in Southern California.** Fred TAYAMA, president of the Los Angeles branch of the J.A.C.L., is reported to be heavily indebted to MUKAEDA and to one Gongoro NAKAMURA (Class "A" suspect), which fact puts these latter two individuals in a position to dictate the policy and action of the local J.A.C.L. through TAYAMA.

NARUMI, Jutaro—Native of Wakayama Prefecture, and believed to be a Japanese citizen, **Class "A" suspect**. For some time he has been manager of the ASIA CO. in Los Angeles. In 1935 was treasurer of the LOS ANGELES JAPANESE CHAMBER OF COMMERCE; for the past several years he has been closely associated with the SAKURA KAI and has been a regular member of the NIPPON KAIGUN KYOKAI. In 1939 he was known to be collecting donations for the Japanese war fund, and in 1940 represented the SUMO KYOKAI [Sumo Wrestling Association] in the local 2600th Anniversary Celebration of the Japanese Empire, held in Los Angeles.

TSUDA, Noboru—Native of Fukushima Prefecture, and probably a Japanese citizen, **Class "A" suspect.** Has been a resident of the United States since 1906, but has made many trips to Japan in the interim and has five sons residing there. Serves as manager and is one of the chief stockholders of the GREAT FUJI (FUJII) THEATER. For some years past he has been very active in Japanese nationalistic organizations and, among other things, was in charge of some of the various Japanese theatrical troupes which came from Japan and toured Hawaii and the West Coast.

In addition to these activities, **TSUDA is a regular member of the suspect NIPPON KAIGUN KYOKAI and is considered by ONI to be a potential Japanese agent**.

UYEDA, Yaozo—Subject himself is treasurer of the NICHIBEI KOGYO KAISHA, and his wife, Yoshiye C. UYEDA, is listed as a member of the suspect NIPPON KAIGUN KYOKAI. (It is believed that subject is actually a member of the latter organization but attempts to hide the fact by having his wife pay his dues.)

BRANCHES:

El Centro	- IWABASHI, Yoshitaro	San Francisco	- YASUMURA, Sadakichi (Class "B" suspect) MIZUNO, Hiroshi (Class "B" suspect)
Guadalupe	- ITO, Setsuji	Suisun	- ISHIBASHI, Chokichi
Lodi	- YAMADA, Tomosaburo	Vallejo	- NAKATA, Manabu
Pismo	- HANAI, Otoichi (Class "B" suspect)	Visalia	- HAGIHARA, Yonekichi
Sacramento	- SERA, Katsutaro NAKASHIMA, Kenkichi		

(All branches are in California, officers as of 1938)

JAPANESE CANNERIES

Alaska and West Coast

OWNERS AND OPERATORS:

ISHIBASHI, "George" Naoichi	-	Portland, Oregon.
NAGAMATSU, "Henry" Heiji	-	Seattle, Washington.
NISHIMURA, "George" Yasukichi	-	Seattle, Washington; and Yokohama, Japan.

SAKAMOTO, Tamizo - Seattle, Washington.

TAKAHASHI, Chas. Theodore (Takeo) - Seattle, Washington.

TAKASAKI, Yaichi (Yoichi) - Kingston, Washington.

SUMMARY:

A comprehensive survey of Japanese activity in the U. S. fishing-canning industry has not yet been made. This present report is merely an account of such circumstances as were revealed through a study of the TOKYO CLUB syndicate.

Reports on hand indicate that Alaskan canneries, whether floating or shore-based, American- or foreign-owned, employ a considerable amount of Japanese capital and labor. Those modern floating canneries based in Japan and their companion fishing fleets are, of course, composed entirely of alien personnel and operate in a manner which permits of very little surveillance on the part of American investigative agencies. Shore-based canneries, on the other hand, are often American-owned but employ laborers of foreign birth or ancestry.

With regard to occupational activity these individuals may be classified as (1) fishermen; (2) "inside" cannery laborers; and (3) superintendents, foremen, carpenters, machinists, etc. In 1939 the above-mentioned cannery labor group numbers some 9,680 workers, of whom the major portion were native Alaskans and Filipinos. The Japanese among them totaled 685 (about 7%), of whom approximately 300 were believed to have returned to Japan at the conclusion of the season. A second detailed check, initiated August, 1941, and still unfinished, shows the proportion of Japanese to be slightly over 6%, or just about what it was in 1939. This percentage is composed almost equally of U.S. citizens and aliens.

American leaders in the fishing-canning industry have endeavored to provide ONI with full information of this situation, stressing the fact that the Japanese involved are scattered in definitely strategic places throughout Alaska, and that there exists the possibility that some of these Japanese, particularly those who go back and forth to Japan, may have Japanese military or naval connections. These allegations are substantiated by reliable reports which specifically refer to suspicious land, sea, and aerial activity in strategic areas by Japanese military or naval officers and others supposedly affiliated with fishing-cannery interests.

Keeping in mind this general background of the situation, one must regard as significant the following data on subject cannery owners and operators and their affiliations. **While there is not sufficient evidence to permit of any blanket or categorical conclusions, the information does appear to suggest an entirely logical connection between the Japanese fishing-cannery interests and other known subversive individuals and organizations.** It is hoped that further investigation will clarify the affiliations and reveal any major Japanese subversion hook-up which may exist.

PERSONNEL:

ISHIBASHI, "George" Naoichi—Alien, **Class "A" suspect. In 1935 was believed to be leader of narcotic smuggling gang as well as a Japanese intelligence agent**. Mail communication with Lt. Comdr. Shigeru FUJII of IJN. In 1941 reported as labor contractor, restaurant owner, and head of KOSHIN CLUB, Portland gambling house affiliated with the TOKYO CLUB chain. Active in Buddhist circles. Intimate with Dr. "Benjamin" Masayoshi TANAKA, Portland Japanese intelligence chief and president of suspect SOKOKU KAI; also close to Kanekichi YAMAMOTO and others of the Seattle TOYO CLUB group.

NAGAMATSU, "Henry" Heiji—Alien, Class "A" suspect. Head of H. H. NAGAMATSU AND COMPANY, cannery contractors, also president-manager of the NORTH COAST IMPORTING COMPANY. Was reported to be a frequent visitor of Kanekichi YAMAMOTO and to be intimately associated with him in cannery union affairs.

NISHIMURA, "George" Yasukichi—Alien, Class "A" suspect. Cannery contractor and operator (plant located at Koguang, Bristol Bay, Alaska) and exporter-importer (owner G. Y. NISHIMURA AND COMPANY, Seattle). Leader of Seattle Japanese. Maintains home in Yokohama to which he used to make annual trips. Heavy contributor to Japanese War Fund. Mail communication (1936–37) with Kanekichi YAMAMOTO, Tamizo SAKAMOTO, and Hakuta FUJIOKA. (All three of these are suspects, YAMAMOTO and SAKAMOTO being active leaders in the TOKYO CLUB chain (see case history on same), as well as having cannery interests; and FUJIOKA, being cannery superintendent for NISHIMURA.) In addition, NISHIMURA was in 1936–37 closely affiliated with Dr. Seiji KANDA (or KONDA), Takuzo SUZUKI, and Koji UCHIDA, Japanese espionage agents who posed as "fishing school instructors" or KYODO SUISAN KAISHA [Marine Cooperative Company] agents while undertaking Alaskan surveys. In April, 1938, was investigated by U. S. Treasury Department on income tax charges, and is believed to have left the country.

SAKAMOTO, Tamizo—Class "A" suspect. Professional gambler, associated with G. Y. NISHIMURA AND COMPANY cannery (manager; also has financial interest). **Prior to 1933** was affiliated with ISHIBASHI and SASAKI in narcotic smuggling. Since 1936 intimate with Lt. Comdr. Shigeru FUJII (IJN; now deceased) and Kanekichi YAMAMOTO. Is reported also as operating a card room in the basement of the L. C. Smith Building, Seattle, said project being backed by the TOYO CLUB (TOKYO CLUB chain) or by YAMAMOTO personally.

TAKAHASHI, Charles Theodore (Takeo)—American-born, **Class "A" suspect.** Wealthy head of C. T. TAKAHASHI COMPANY, an export-import firm dealing mostly in lumber and scrap metal and formerly known as the ORIENTAL TRADING COMPANY. (Same firm is sometimes called the CHINA IMPORT AND EXPORT COMPANY, probably with the intention of hiding its Japanese ownership.) Also head of RESILIENT H???ER, INC., AND O. T. CONTRACTORS, INC., the latter supplying labor to fisheries, lumber camps, and railroads. All of these firms are reported to be fronts for widespread and diversified activity of a subversive nature; contacts and affiliations and known Japanese and Occidental pro-Nazi elements in the U. S. and Mexico have been both consistent and of long standing.

TAKAHASHI himself does considerable travel, frequently to Japan, and acts as go-between in arranging for so-called "inspection trips" to important plants, airports, strategic areas, etc., by visiting Japanese military-naval officers and business men. Over a long period he was in intimate contact with such key men as Colonel Usaburo OKA, Inspector of the Imperial Japanese Army Ordnance Inspector's Office in New

York City, Commanders Shigeru FUJII and Taro ISOBE, IJN, and also Majors Otoji NISHIMURA and Munemichi TONAMI (now Lt. Col.). He was also reported to have been a silent partner of Kanekichi YAMAMOTO in the TOKYO CLUB chain prior to the latter's deportation from this country in 1939. Other activities of interest are his recent concentration upon the purchase of apartment houses and hotels in and about Seattle, and his apparent assumption of control of Mitsubishi (Seattle branch) funds for the duration of the "freezing order."

TAKASAKI, Yaichi (or Yoichi)—Alien, Class "A" suspect. During the fishing season is employed as cannery foreman by G. Y. NISHIMURA COMPANY of Seattle. Little else is known of him except for his connection with sumo, or Japanese wrestling.

JAPANESE CANNERIES—Supplement

TAKAMOTO, Felix (with aliases Felix QUINAL, Marsek QUINAL) and Mary TAKAMOTO (alias Mary QUINAL)—Felix is believed to be a Malayan with some Japanese blood. Both subjects are known active Communist organizers in the fish canneries at Terminal Island, California. They are also reported to act as go-betweens for certain Japanese organizations and members of the fishing fleet believed to be engaged in subversive activities off the Mexican Coast.

HOSHI, Hiroshi ("Paul")—An American-born Japanese, age 26, HOSHI is considered a dangerous suspect and has been recommended for custodial detention. **In 1933**, he was reported to be President of the SEATTLE JAPANESE AMATEUR RADIO CLUB and operator of Station W7CFJ. He was employed in 1937 as operator for the Van Camp Sea Food Company's fishing boat SAN RAFAEL, based at San Diego.

In the **summer of 1938** he was reported to be an officer and member of ARTA, American Radio Telegraphists Association (C.I.O.), and also to be acting as a contact man between the Communist Party, the C.I.O. and the Japanese in the fishing industry. At this time, he was employed as radio operator on the Van Camp Co.'s boat DESTINY. In the winter of **1940** he was reportedly employed as radio operator on the SANTA INEZ operating between San Diego and Mexico.

ALASKA CANNERY WORKERS UNION

(A. F. of L. Affiliate, Local #2054)
519 Main Street
Seattle, Washington

OFFICERS:

ARAI, Clarence T.	-	One-time leader and organizer (1937).
OKAZAKI, "Robert" I.	-	President (1937–38).
WATANABE, Yozo	-	Organizer and president (1937).

(Recent officers not reported.)

SUMMARY:

When last reported (**1938**), the 200–300 membership of this union was mostly Japanese. Like its rival, the C. I. O. Local #7 (see case history), the group is apparently connected, through the Japanese Consulates and Japanese labor and cannery contractors (see case history on JAPANESE CANNERIES), with large-scale fishing-cannery interests which are known to be deeply involved in various types of subversive activity. It might also be noted that the A. F. of L. union, in a test of strength wherein the bargaining agency of the salmon packing industry was at stake, lost to the C. I. O. group, and has since been definitely subordinate as a representative group.

It is felt that description of the interlocking affiliations of those who once held key positions in the union will do more to identify the exact nature of the organization than will any further general statement.

MEMBERS:

ARAI, Clarence T.—**Class "A" suspect**, Captain U.S.A. Reserves (commission expired 6/1/41). Prominent attorney and civic leader in Seattle. Local leader (and one-time national head) of the JAPANESE AMERICAN CITIZENS LEAGUE, also of the ALASKA CANNERY WORKERS UNION, which union he helped organize. Has had active contacts with influential Japanese Army, Navy, and consular officials over a long period (Major TAKAHASHI and Consul OKAMOTO among others) and is reported to travel extensively. **It is also worth noting that**

a 1936 report records the belief that ARAI was a member of an exceedingly clever and astute intelligence ring, and that inquiry into the case at that time was not advisable.

KANAYA, Richard T.—One of the organizers of the ALASKA CANNERY WORKERS UNION; at present an officer of the ASSOCIATION OF JAPANESE CANNERY WORKERS, which was recently organized to supplant the so-called "JAPANESE EDUCATIONAL SOCIETY." (The ASSOCIATION OF JAPANESE CANNERY WORKERS apparently aims to unite both A. F. L. and C. I. O. labor union members under Japanese control. See case history on the association.)

MATSUMOTO, Ken—One-time officer in the TOKYO CLUB syndicate (see case history) and interested, with Kanekichi YAMAMOTO and others in the syndicate, in the formation of the ALASKA CANNERY WORKERS UNION.

NAGAMATSU, "Henry" Heiji—Class "A" suspect, Japanese citizen. Head of the H. H. NAGAMATSU AND COMPANY, cannery contractors; also president-manager of the NORTH COAST IMPORTING COMPANY, both of Seattle. Was observed to be a frequent visitor of Kanekichi YAMAMOTO and is believed to be involved, through YAMAMOTO and his own work as a labor contractor, in the affairs of the ALASKA CANNERY WORKERS UNION.

NISHIMURA, "George" Yasukichi—Class "A" suspect. Cannery contractor and operator (plant located at Koguang, Bristol Bay, Alaska) and exporter-importer (owner G. Y. NISHIMURA AND COMPANY, Seattle). Leader of Seattle Japanese. Maintains home in Yokohama to which he used to make annual trips. Heavy contributor to Japanese War Fund. Mail communication (**1936–37**) with Kanekichi YAMAMOTO, Tamizo SAKAMOTO, and Hakuta FUJIOKA. (All three of these are suspects, YAMAMOTO and SAKAMOTO being active leaders in the TOKYO CLUB chain (see case history on same), as well as having cannery interests; and FUJIOKA, being cannery superintendent for NISHIMURA.) In addition, NISHIMURA was in **1936–37** closely affiliated with Dr. Seiji KANDA (or KONDA), Takuzo SUZUKI, and Koji UCHIDA, Japanese espionage agents who posed as "fishing school instructors" or KYODO SUISAN KAISHA agents while undertaking Alaskan surveys. In April, 1938, was investigated by U. S. Treasury Department on income tax charges, and is believed to have left the country.

OKAZAKI, "Robert" Iwao—Was president of the ALASKA CANNERY WORKERS UNION in **1937–1938. Nothing known to ONI of his earlier background.** In 1939 was contacted in Los Angeles by M. A. AKIYAMA, who was reported as having just come from Japan on a "secret mission."

WATANABE, Yozo—Class "A" suspect. One of the original organizers and one-time president (**1937**) of the ALASKA CANNERY WORKERS UNION; owner of a Seattle clothes cleaning and pressing shop. In frequent telephonic communication with Kanekichi YAMAMOTO, to whom he is alleged to have reported union affairs.

YAMAMOTO, Kanekichi—Class "A" suspect. **Until 1938** was one of the leaders in the TOKYO CLUB chain (see case history); was also affiliated with the NICHIBEI KOGYO KAISHA (see case history).

He has long been interested in cannery business and is reported to have been one of the chief forces behind the formation of the ALASKA CANNERY WORKERS UNION. Frequently in the company of Lt. Commander Shigeru FUJII, IJN, and Consul Issaku OKAMOTO. Deported in 1939, and at present believed to be in Shanghai (perhaps operating the Chinese branches of the TOKYO CLUB gambling-smuggling syndicate).

CANNERY WORKERS AND FARM LABORERS UNION

(CIO Affiliate, Local #7)
Seattle, Washington

OFFICERS:

HAMA, Carl (Aliases: YONEDA, Karl or George; HAMA, Kiyoshi; UCHIDA, Tsutomo.)	- Vice President (1939).
ITO, Kenji (or Kenzo)	- Legal representative (1941).

KUMAMOTO, Yukio	- Member Executive Board (1937–1938).
MINATO, "George" Masao	- Delegate (1938) to national convention of the UNITED CANNERY, AGRICULTURAL, PACKING AND ALLIED WORKERS OF AMERICA.
MIYAGAWA, "Dyke" Daisuke	- Member Executive Board (1937–1938) in charge of publicity.
TAKIGAWA, "George"	- Vice President (1937–1938) and delegate to national convention of the UCAPAWA (1938).

SUMMARY:

As stated in the report on JAPANESE CANNERIES (see case history), the interests of cannery laborers are represented by the A.F. of L. ALASKA CANNERY WORKERS UNION and the above-mentioned CIO CANNERY WORKERS AND FARM LABORERS UNION. Of these two unions the latter is by far the larger and more influential; at the same time both groups are related through a newly organized ASSOCIATION OF JAPANESE CANNERY WORKERS (see case history), which ostensibly aims to consolidate the Japanese elements into a united labor front.

While the Japanese membership of subject union (1939 total about 700) is numerically inferior to the Filipino, it is obvious that the Japanese are in control of key positions and have utilized the union as a front for activities far removed from the demands of normal cannery business. An inspection of the attached diagram and a study of the individual affiliations set forth below will indicate that the union's connections with the West Coast Japanese consulates, Army and Navy agents, officials of the TOKYO CLUB chain, and other suspects have been more than coincidental. It must constantly be kept in mind in this connection that Japan strove to put into operation in the United States and its territories a highly integrated and specialized intelligence network which could "take over" from regular established agencies in wartime.

Under such circumstances, Japanese nationals and pro-Japanese nisei who are well settled in normal and yet strategic occupations are likely to be the mainstay of Japanese espionage-sabotage operations in this country.

MEMBERS AND ASSOCIATES:

HAMA, Carl (with aliases)—Class "A" suspect. West Coast Communist Party organizer and labor agitator. Editor (1936) of the San Francisco HODO SHIMBUN, a Communist Japanese-language news organ (no longer published); contributor (1941) to the Communist DOHO newspaper of Los Angeles, which is also printed (in English) by Japanese. Credited with having organized the Los Angeles JAPANESE WORKERS ASSOCIATION in **1936**. Active in AMERICAN LEAGUE AGAINST WAR AND FASCISM. Vice president of subject union in 1939.

ITO, Kenji (or Kenzo)—Nisei (second generation) Japanese, Class "A" suspect. Active in JACL (1935–). One-time Japanese Consul at New Orleans and, since **October, 1937**, legal adviser and "special member" of the Seattle Consulate assigned to propaganda. Was reported in April, 1941, to be legal representative of subject labor union. Extremely active since **1937** as propagandist defending Japanese foreign policy; reported for naval espionage in 1940. He has done extensive traveling in the U. S. and Latin America as well as in the Orient.

KUMAMOTO, Yukio—A U. S. citizen, Class "A" suspect. Former president of the Seattle chapter of the KIBEI NIKKEI SHIMIN KYOKAI (a society composed of American-born Japanese who have been brought up and educated in Japan from childhood until majority). Office manager of Seattle Branch of MITSUBISHI SHOJI KAISHA until very recently. Member of the Executive Board of subject CANNERY WORKERS AND FARM LABORERS UNION, Local #7.

MINATO, "George" Masao—Formerly student at University of Washington. In 1938 made unsuccessful bid for office in subject union; was, however, elected delegate to national convention that year. Has short wave radio license (W-7-FNG). Treasurer (1941), ASSOCIATION OF JAPANESE CANNERY WORKERS (see case history).

MIYAGAWA, "Dyke" Daisuke—American-educated nisei, suspected of membership in the Communist Party. Has for some time been striving to consolidate the West Coast Japanese into a political bloc to exploit the power he feels due them. Member (1937–1938) of Executive Board of subject union, in charge of publicity. President (1941) of ASSOCIATION OF JAPANESE CANNERY WORKERS (see case history).

OKAMARU. "Welley" or Welly" Shoji—American-educated Nisei (with Kibei classification), Class "A" espionage suspect. Reported (July, 1941) to have repudiated his American citizenship. For the past six or seven years has been in the Japanese Consular Service (Seattle), first as Secretary, then as Consular Assistant and more recently as Chancellor. Is known to have cooperated closely with Lt. Comdr. Sadatomo OKADA and Chancellor Kanji KANEKO (both of Seattle) in the local Japanese intelligence system; OKAMARU is reported to head a unit which contacts labor unions, particularly members of the Communist party in the A.F. of L. and C.I.O.

TAKIGAWA, "George" Kiyoshi—American-educated Nisei, active as political and labor leader among West Coast second-generation Japanese. Vice president of subject CANNERY WORKERS AND FARM LABORERS UNION, Local 07, and delegate to the 1938 national convention. President of the JAPANESE EDUCATIONAL SOCIETY from **1938 or 1939** until the dissolution of the society in 1941. (TAKIGAWA was actually forced to resign sometime before the group disbanded, having been charged with conduct unsupportable by the organization and specifically with having accepted money in return for job favors. The society was then reorganized and renamed the ASSOCIATION OF JAPANESE CANNERY WORKERS.)

TAKIGAWA (or TAKI), William—Class "B" Nisei suspect, brother of "George" Kiyoshi TAKIGAWA. Believed to be either a Communist party member or a "fellow-traveler;" has done some work among the Negroes. Was an unsuccessful candidate for office in subject union in **1939**. Has done some traveling between Seattle and Alaska.

ASSOCIATION OF JAPANESE CANNERY WORKERS

(Formerly the Japanese Educational Society)

Seattle, Washington

OFFICERS:

MIYAGAWA, "Dyke" Daisuke	-	President
KANAZAWA, Hiroshi	-	Secretary
MINATO, "George" Masao	-	Treasurer
OKAMOTO, Eddie M.	-	Trustee
UYENO, Tom	-	Trustee
HIRAHARA, Davis	-	Member of Advisory Board
KANAYA, Richard T.	-	Member of Advisory Board
KAWANO, M.	-	Member of Advisory Board
KIKUCHI, Chihiro	-	Member of Advisory Board
MIYAMOTO, Frank	-	Member of Advisory Board
OKAZAKI, Masayuki	-	Member of Advisory Board
WATANABE, Taul	-	Member of Advisory Board

SUMMARY:

Subject association was originally known as the JAPANESE EDUCATIONAL SOCIETY, and under that title functioned as a headquarters for Japanese aliens and Nisei connected with the canning business. President of the JAPANESE EDUCATIONAL SOCIETY during the three years of its existence (1938–1941) was "George" Kiyoshi TAKIGAWA (see case history on CANNERY WORKERS AND FARM LABORERS UNION, C.I.O. Local #7). He was forced to resign his office shortly before the group was dissolved, having been charged with "conduct unsupportable by the organization," and specifically with having accepted money in return for job favors.

Information is lacking to indicate whether or not the JAPANESE EDUCATIONAL SOCIETY had membership covering the A. F. of L.

ALASKA CANNERY WORKERS UNION as well as the aforementioned C.I.O. group, but the newly formed organization (viz. The ASSOCIATION OF JAPANESE CANNERY WORKERS) is definitely known to cover both unions. (It should be noted that, while these unions are predominantly of native Alaskan and Filipino membership, the Japanese manage to retain a large measure of control. Union affiliation with Japanese consulates and other Japanese offices or agents are described in the case histories of the respective unions.)

MEMBERS' AFFILIATIONS:

MIYAGAWA, "Dyke" Daisuke—American-educated Nisei (second generation Japanese), active in political and labor spheres among the West Coast Japanese. Is suspected of Communist affiliations, though his membership in the CP has not been definitely ascertained. Has been a member of the Executive Board of the C.I.O. CANNERY WORKERS AND FARM LABORERS UNION, Local #7, in charge of publicity (1937–1939).

MINATO, "George" Masao—American-educated nisei. Has short wave radio license (W-7-FNG). Delegate of the C.I.O. CANNERY WORKERS AND FARM LABORERS UNION, Local #7, to the international convention of the UNITED CANNERY, AGRICULTURAL, PACKING AND ALLIED WORKERS OF AMERICA at San Francisco (**December 1938**).

MIYAMOTO, Frank Shotaro—American-educated Nisei, instructor in sociology at the University of Washington (1941). Has done considerable research on sociological conditions among Japanese in the Seattle area. Worked in Alaska the summer of 1941 (exact duties unknown). Nothing of a derogatory nature has yet been reported concerning him. (It may be possible that this is not the same Frank MIYAMOTO listed above under "Officers.")

KANAYA, Richard T.—One of the speakers at the first organization meeting of the A.F. of L. ALASKA CANNERY WORKERS UNION.

UYENO, Tom—One of twenty-one delegates of the C.I.O. CANNERY WORKERS AND FARM LABORERS UNION, Local #7, to the Washington State C.I.O. Convention (**1938**).

HOTELS INVOLVED IN TOKYO CLUB SYNDICATE

HOLLAND HOTEL 504 Fourth Avenue Seattle, Washington	- MINAMI, S.—Manager prior to 1/14/41 LARKIN, —)—Present managers (1/14/41) VERNON, —)
KASHU HOTEL 1701 Laguna Street San Francisco, California	- NAKANO, Sakutaro—Owner (August, 1941) Class "A" suspect
N. P. HOTEL 306 Sixth Avenue, S. Seattle, Washington	- SHITAMAE, Niroku "Frank"—Senior partner SHITAMAE, Shihei "George"—Brother and joint operator (2/27/41) N. S. INVESTMENT CO. (believed to be operated by SHITAMAE BROS.)—Owner (1/14/41)
OHIO HOTEL 1215 S. W. Front St. Portland, Oregon	- SUMIDA, James Yoshio—Lessee
OLYMPIC HOTEL (also referred to as NEW OLYMPIC HOTEL) 117 N. San Pedro St. Los Angeles, Calif.	- SAWANO, J.—(Contact man)—Manager (**May, 1935**) WATANABE, Kyohei—(Contact man and agent)—Assistant manager (May, 1935) FUKUI, Soji (Soki)—Organizer and stock-holder (9/15/36)
PORTLAND HOTEL	- Location and management unknown
S. P. HOTEL 123 West Burnside Ave. Portland, Oregon	- SUMIDA, James Yoshio—Lessee
STEVENS HOTEL	- Location and management unknown

TACOMA HOTEL 822 Jackson Street Seattle, Washington	-	HARA, Seiichi)—"Hotel partners" (1/30/41) KAWAKAMI, Kakuzo) (Another report (1/14/41) lists HARA, Seiichi—Manager WAHLSTROM (Mrs.)—Owner)
U. S. HOTEL 315 Maynard Street Seattle, Washington	-	MIYAGAWA, "Joe" Genke—Manager (6/3/41) Is the brother of the MIYAGAWA (probably "Dyke" Daisuke) who owns GOLDEN DONUT CAFE PRENTISS REALTY CO.—Owner (1/14/41)

RESTAURANTS, CAFES, CLUBS, AND POOL HALLS INVOLVED IN TOKYO CLUB SYNDICATE

The FRISCO CAFE 560 Fifth Avenue San Diego, California	-	
GOLDEN DONUT CAFE Seattle, Washington	-	MIYAGAWA, "Dyke" Daisuke—Owner (6/3/41)
KOSHIN CLUB Portland, Oregon	-	ISHIBASHI, "George" Naoichi—Proprietor (1941)
NEW CENTRAL CAFE 653 Weller St. Seattle, Washington	-	FURUMOTO, S. (Mrs.)—Proprietor (1941)
NIPPON POOL HALL 608 Main Street Seattle, Washington	-	SAITO, Moriya (Dr.)—Owner (1941)

The SHINKO CLUB 1725 Laguna Street San Francisco, California	- YASUMURA, Sadakichi—Manager (4/22/38)
STACY STREET TAVERN 2401 First Ave., S. (corner of Stacy St.) Seattle, Washington	- ASAKURA, Makutaro—Proprietor (1/30/41)
The STAR POOL HALL 517 Jackson Street Seattle, Washington	- ICHIKAWA, Hakui—Proprietor (11/4/41)
The SUN CAFE 421 Market Street San Diego, California	- OBAYASHI, J. U.—Operator (1940)
TOKYO CAFE 239 Elm Ave. Long Beach, California	-

To: All Naval Districts except ND 6, FBI, MID, COI, State Dept., Special Defense Unit of Dept. of Justice

Appendix 3

Crystal City Registry Japanese Family List
February 11, 1945

Beginning in 1942 to 1948 about six thousand internees were incarcerated at Crystal City internment Camp located one hundred and twenty miles south of San Antonio, Texas. The Camp held Japanese, German and Italian immigrants, their families and American born children. It also interned many from Latin America.

The Camp was known as a "family internment camp" but it was FDR'S center for his secret prisoner exchange program. For many it could be described as a kidnap camp.

Enclosed is the Crystal City register prepared and compiled in detail by Japanese inmates themselves. It is perhaps the only English copy of such information. It includes past and previous addresses, ages, names of family members and occupation of inmates . . . all those from Hawaii, US mainland and Latin American Countries. It provides invaluable information of people who were "exchanged" and sent to Japan. Some, like Frank Nagashima who helped make available this list, were able to make it back. Others were not. They were children of parents who remained in Japan. These children have a right to seek remedies against the US government.

In the case of Hawaii, for example, we can count 104 innocent children abandoned behind the enemy line. An inexcusable tactic committed by FDR and the US Government. Many of such children are still alive, living somewhere in Japan. Their rights have been abrogated and need to be restored.

CRYSTAL CITY REGISTRY JAPANESE FAMILY LIST February 11 1945

Compiled by the Governing Body of Crystal City Camp and made available in mimeograph form to all inmates.

Translated by Kumiko Yamabe and edited by Claude Morita

Name (Age)	Primary Address	Previous Address	Occupation	Section No.
(A)				
ABE, Naoji (25)	Yasuhara-cho, Date-gun, Fukushima Pref.	Lima, Peru, South America	Hardware seller	Q-69-2
	*Family * wife: Miki, first daughter: Kyoko			
ABE, Tatsuo (40)	Segami-cho, Nobuo-gun, Fukushima Pref.	San Bernadino, California	Business	T-4-A
	*Family * wife: Yukie, first son: Shizuo, first daughter: Yaeko, Second daughter: Nobuko			
ABE, Toyoji (64)	Higashisakae-mura, Tagawa-gun, Yaamagata Pref.	San Francisco, California	Newspaper	D-9-A
	*Family * wife: Yuka, forth daughter: Hana			
AGEMURA, Masanuki (41)	Makurazaki-cho, Kawabe-gun, Kagoshima Pref.	Delano, California	Agriculture	D-13-A
	*Family * wife: Sakiko, first son: Hiroshi, second son: Ikuto, first daughter: Yoko			

AIDA, Kinzou (40)	Shiun-ji, Kita kamohara-gun, Nigata Pref.	Lima, Peru, South America	Cleaning	Q-61-1
	*Family * second son: Esao, third son: Tokio			
AKAHORI, Sai (60)	Sana kawachi-mura, Meito-gun, Tokushima Pref.	Seattle, Washington	Newspaper writer	Q-53-4
	*Family * wife: Kikuko, first daughter: Tomoko			
AKASHI, Yuichi (48)	Nishikawa-mura, Kume-gun, Okayama Pref.	Lima, Peru, South America	Agriculture	T-27-A
	*Family * wife: Mutsu, first son: Hiroyuki, first daughter: Tomoko, second daughter: Yaeko			
AKIYAMA, Masao (38)	Eimei-mura, Yushuku-gun, Kagoshima Pref.	San Francisco, California	Restaurant	T-6-C
	*Family * wife: Chiyoko			
AKIYAMA, Michiharu (50)	Seigoku-mura, Kodo-gun, Hiroshima Pref.	Florence, California	Business	D-18-A
	*Family * wife: Onatsu, first son: Ichiro, third son: Ryozo, fourth son: Shiro			
ANDO, Soukichi (58)	Aito-mura, Honsu-gun, Gifu Pref.	Tracy, California	Agriculture	D-29-B
	*Family * wife: Kiku, first son: Souji, second son: Yoshinosuke, first daughter: Mikie			

(continued)

CRYSTAL CITY REGISTRY JAPANESE FAMILY LIST February 11 1945 *(continued)*

Name (Age)	Primary Address	Previous Address	Occupation	Section No.
AOKI, Yoshiichi (69)	Ota-mura, Azuma-gun, Gunma Pref.	Sacramento, California	Business	T-36-B
	*Family * wife: Masa			
AOKI, Kamenosuke (64)	Shimoya-ku, Naganegishi, Tokyo	Huntington Beach, California	Agriculture	T-39-A
	*Family * wife: Iku, second daughter: Yaeko			
AOKI, Kanya (40)	Iri arai, Ohmori-ku, Tokyo	La Paz, Bolivia, South America	Business	T-1-BC
	*Family * wife: Tomi, first son: Jyouya, second son: Nobuya, fourth son: Shiro			
AOYAGI, Fusaku (38)	Iribe-mura, Sagara-gun, Fukuoka Pref.	Chiclayo, Peru, South America	Business	D-34-A
	*Family * wife: Kiyoko, first son: Tatsuo, second son: Tekio, first daughter: Nobuko			
ARAKI, Masao (42)	Kawaguchi-mura, Hotaku-gun, Kumamoto Pref.	Fresno, California	Teacher	EQ-79-4
	*Family * wife: Shizuko, first daughter: Yumiko			
ARAMAKI, Kameki (54)	Hiroyasu-mura, Kamiasushiro-gun, Kumamoto Pref.	Watsonville, California	Business	Q-48-1
	*Family * wife: Yoneko, first son: Shouji, second son: Kazutoshi, first daughter: Akiko, mother-in-law: KICHIJI, Momoki			

ARIKAWA, Sadao (59)	Kajiki-cho, Shira-gun, Kagoshima Pref.	Long Beach, California	Insurance company	T-29-C
	*Family * wife: Masae			
ARIMA, Sumio (43)	Shiroyama-cho, Nakano-ku, Tokyo	Seattle, Washington	Newspaper	T-19-AC
	*Family * wife: Fujio; first son: Sumiyasu; second son: Sumimasa; first daughter: Eiko; second daughter: Mutsuko; third daughter: Noriko			
ARIMOTO, Masazou (55)	Chikushiro-mura, Chikujyou-gun, Fukuoka Pref.	San Bernadino, California	Business	T-59-B
	*Family * wife: Kimiko, first son: Masaaki			
ARITA, Kouzou (58)	Shiida-cho, Chikujyou-gun, Fukuoka Pref.	Lanai, Hawaii	Barber	V-151-A
	*Family * wife: Kimiko			
ASANO, Masaaki (39)	Yoshifuji-mura, Kita Uwa-gun, Ehime Pref.	Kohala, Hawaii	Missionary	T-8-A
	*Family * wife: Takako, first son: Yoshikatsu, second son: Fumitaka, first daughter: Hiromi			
ASE, Seikichi (59)	Date-mura, Aritama-gun, Hokkaido	Niland, California	Professor	D-3-A
	*Family * wife: Toyo, second son: Kiyoshi, third son: Kiyoto; first daughter: Naoko; second daughter: Seiko			

(*continued*)

CRYSTAL CITY REGISTRY JAPANESE FAMILY LIST February 11 1945 *(continued)*

Name (Age)	Primary Address	Previous Address	Occupation	Section No.
ASHIZAWA, Koshin (Shigeru) (52)	Hikawa-mura, Higashi Yamanashi-gun, Yamanashi Pref.	San Francisco, California	Cleaning	T-59-C
	*Family * wife: Masano			
(D)				
DEKI, Ichiro (50)	Sakai-machi, Takatsuji-dori, Kyoto	Oahu, Hawaii	Photo studio	T-17-A
	*Family * wife: Harue, first son: Shuichi, first daughter: Toshie			
DODOUHARA, Hiroo (52)	Yasu-mura, Asa-gun, Hiroshima Pref.	Lima, Peru, South America	Merchant	EQ-84-3
	*Family * wife: Takeno, first son: Takashi, second son: Tamotsu, third son: Hiroshi, first daughter: Masako			
DOIGUCHI, Yutaro (58)	Yamataki-gun, Senboku-gun, Osaka	San Francisco, California	Transportation agent	Q-43-3
	*Family * wife: Shizuko, first daughter: Etsuko			
Cho, Tsutomu (57)	Numabe-gun, Tooda-gun, Miyagi Pref.	Santa Barbara, California	Agriculture	Q-51-1
	*Family * wife: Masayo, first son: Ken, second son: Tadashi, nephew: Hajime, niece: Chieko			

(E)				
ENDO, Fumio (38)	Kaminagai, Minami Okiba-gun, Yamagata Pref.	Lima, Peru, South America	Business	D-44-A
	*Family * wife: Makiko, first son: Hisashi; second daughter: Teruko; third daughter: Mitsuko			
(F)				
FUJIHANA, Masamichi (40)	Nakazato-cho, Takinokawa-ku, Tokyo	Maui, Hawaii	Missionary	T-56-A
	*Family * wife: Hisa; first son: Michihiko; second son: Teruhiko; third son: Yoshihiko			
FUJII, Hisashi (38)	Goso-mura, Kawakami-gun, Okayama Pref.	Lima, Peru, South America	Business	T-13-BC
	*Family * wife: Sumiko; first son: Hidetoshi; first daughter: Michiko; second daughter: Haruko; third daughter: Yoshiko			
FUJII, Tatsutomo (53)	Taira-mura, Saeki-gun, Hiroshima Pref.	Clovis, California	Missionary	T-53-B
	*Family * wife: Kushino; first son: Tetsuro			
FUJII, Hishitarou (44)	Arita-mura, Nishimui-gun, Wakayama Pref.	Seattle, Washington	Merchant	Q-40-2
	*Family * wife: Misaho, first son: Susumu; first daughter: Hatsue; second daughter: Reiko			

(*continued*)

CRYSTAL CITY REGISTRY JAPANESE FAMILY LIST February 11 1945 *(continued)*

Name (Age)	Primary Address	Previous Address	Occupation	Section No.
FUJII, Shigetoshi (48)	Yashiro-mura, Tohaku-gun, Tottori Pref.	Los Angeles, California	Greenhouse	T-46-A
	*Family * wife: Kikuyo; third son: Nao; first daughter: Aiko			
FUJIIKE, Tamotsu (43)	Matsuzaki-cho, Kamo-gun, Shizuoka Pref.	La Paz, Bolivia, South America	Business	T-2-AC
	*Family * wife: Take; first son: Yasuo; third son: Toshio; first daughter: Masako; second daughter: Hiroko; adopted daughter: SATO, Hatsue			
FUJIKADO, Yoshinobu (34)	Arima-cho, Minami takaki-gun, Nagasaki Pref.	Salinas, California	Missionary	EQ-83-4
	*Family * wife: Matsue; first son: Shinya			
FUJISAWA, Hideo (48)	Sanbongi-cho, Hida-gun, Miyagi Pref.	Honolulu, Hawaii	Missionary	T-45-A
	*Family * wife: Aiko; first son: Hiroyuki; first daughter: Shizuko			
FUKUBA, Tosuke (63)	Mirasaka-cho, Sosan-gun, Hiroshima Pref.	Watsonville, California	Agriculture	Q-66-4
	*Family * wife: Kikuno			

FUKUDA, Teiichiro (59)	Nabe-mura, Tamana-gun, Kumamoto Pref.	Oahu, Hawaii	Teacher	D-59-B
	*Family * wife: Kimi; first daughter: Fumiko; second daughter: Yukiko; third daughter: Yayoi			
FUKUDA, Yoshiaki (46)	Kamikita-mura, Yoshino-gun, Nara Pref.	San Francisco, California	Priest of Kinko-kyo	D-11-A
	*Family * wife: Mako; first son: Michiaki; second son: Nobuaki; third son: Saburo; fourth son: Yoshiro; fifth son: Hiroshi; sixth son:Koichi; first daughter: Makiko			
FUKUNAGA, Yutaka (38)	Higashi kokubu-mura, Shira-gun, Kagoshima Pref.	Gardena, California	Broker	D-8-B
	*Family * wife: Chiyoko; first daughter: Takako; second daughter: Kyoko; third daughter: Teruyo.			
FUKUSHIMA, Gunichi (60)	Kuchi-mura, Asa-gun, Hiroshima Pref.	Dinuba, California	Agriculture	D-19-AB
	*Family * wife: Kame; first son: Jyoji; second son: Haruo; fifth son: Yoshinori; first daughter: Yoshie; second daughter: Takako; third daughter: Sachiko; fourth daughter: Shigeko			
FUKUSHIMA, Hama (59)	Tsunaki-mura, Ihoku-gun, Kumamoto Pref.	Terminal Island, California	Missionary	T-31-B
	*Family * none			
FUNO, Mitsuzou (45)	Tashiro-cho, Chigusa-ku, Nagoya-city, Aichi Pref.	Seattle, Washington	Missionary	EQ-93-3
	*Family * wife: Ushie; first son: Masatada; first daughter: Michiyo			

(*continued*)

CRYSTAL CITY REGISTRY JAPANESE FAMILY LIST February 11 1945 *(continued)*

Name (Age)	Primary Address	Previous Address	Occupation	Section No.
FURUMOTO, Souichi (52)	Edajima-mura, Aki-gun, Hiroshima Pref.	Woodland, California	Agriculture	T-30-A
	*Family * wife: Momoyo, first san: Akio; second son: Minoru; first daughter: Keiko; second daughter: Ruiko			
FURUSAWA, Takashi (69)	Uchiyamashita-cho, Okayama-city, Okayama Pref.	Los Angeles, California	Doctor	D-57-B
	*Family * wife: Sachiko			
FURUTA, Ichiro (40)	Gono-mura, Fukayasu-gun, Hiroshima Pref.	Walnut Grove, California	Agriculture	T-40-A
	*Family * wife: Chiyoko; first daughter: Kikue; second daughter: Midori			
FURUYA, Sadayasu (43)	Kashiwa-mura, Higashiyashiro-gun, Yamanashi Pref.	Suisun, California	Agriculture	T-55-C
	*Family * wife: Fumi			
(G)				
GIMA, Masafuku (47)	Tamaki-mura, Shimajiri-gun, Okinawa Pref.	Honolulu, Hawaii	Doctor	T-13-A
	*Family * wife: Tsuruko; first son: Tadashi; first daughter: Michiko			

GOURO, Kenzou (53)	Tawara-mura, Kamo-gun, Hiroshima Pref.	Piula, Peru, South America	Business	T-8-EC
	*Family * wife: Yone; third son: Tadao; second daughter: Sueyo; third daughter: Noriko; fourth daughter: Hanae			
GOSHO, Hiroshi (51)	Uchide-cho, Ashiya-city, Hyogo Pref.	Seattle, Washington	Pharmacist	T-42-B
	*Family * wife: Shizuko, first daughter: Tazuko			
GOUDA, Fumio (41)	Yoshizaka-mura, Yamagata-gun, Hiroshima Pref.	Monterey, California	Business	T-41-B
	*Family * wife: Toshiko; first son: Akira			
GOTO, Hirado (65)	Kawachi-mura, Hotaku-gun, Kumamoto Pref.	Torujillo, Peru, South America	Fabric shop	Q-56-2
	*Family * wife: Jyuki			
GOTO, Tokiyoshi (44)	Kawachi-mura, Hotaku-gun, Kumamoto Pref.	Torjillo, Peru, South America	Fabric shop	Q-56-1
	*Family * wife: Kinue; first son: Toru; first daughter: Michiko; second daughter: Fumiko			
GUSHI, Yukinobu (40)	Nago-cho, Kokutou-gun, Okinawa Pref.	Lima, Peru, South America	Agriculture	DV-105-B
	*Family * wife: Chiru; first son: Yukihide; first daughter: Setsuko; second daughter: Emiko; third daughter: Nobuko			

(*continued*)

CRYSTAL CITY REGISTRY JAPANESE FAMILY LIST February 11 1945 *(continued)*

Name (Age)	Primary Address	Previous Address	Occupation	Section No.
GUSHIKEN, Hironobu (44)	Honbu-cho, Kokutou-gun, Okinawa Pref.	Oatvilles, Texas	Agriculture	D-28-B
	*Family * wife: Tsune; first son: Hiroaki; first daughter: Keiko; second daughter: Harue			
GUSHIKEN, Kohei (41)	Honbu-cho, Kokutou-gun, Okinawa Pref.	Lima, Peru, South America	Clothing seller	Q-65-1
	*Family * wife: Nobuko			
GUSHIKEN, Kyouho (44)	Nago-cho, Kokutou-gun, Okinawa Pref.	Lima, Peru, South America	Agriculture	DV-149-A
	*Family * wife: Sakiko; first son: Kou; second son: Takeshi; third son: Hitoshi; first daughter: Shouko; father-in-law: KANESHIRO, Fukusuke			
(H)				
HACHIYA, Hiroshi (39)	Higashisene-mura, Kanzaki-gun, Saga Pref.	Wankayo, Peru, South America	Material shop	Q-84-1
	*Family * wife: Michi; first son: Masayuki; first daughter: Yasuko; second daughter: Kesami; third daughter: Yemi			

HOUGA, Isao (44)	Date-cho, Date-gun, Fukushima Pref.	Gardena, California	Greenhouse	D-4-A
	*Family * wife: Yoshiko, second son: Hideyo, third son: Tadashi, first daughter: Keiko, second daughter: Mikiko			
HAMA, Hideo (44)	Ohmoto-mura, Okayama-city, Okayama Pref.	Seward, Alaska	Judo Instructor	T-42-A
	*Family * wife: Hisa; first son: Masato; second son: Masayuki; father-in-law: KUMASHIRO, Otogorou			
HAMADA, Otoshirou (34)	Esumi-mura, Nishimui-gun, Wakayama Pref.	Honolulu, Hawaii	Househusband	V-133-B
	*Family * wife: Harue; first son: Kouji			
HAMAGUCHI, Sadakichi (42)	Shimosato-cho, Higashimui-gun, Wakayama Pref.	Monterey, California	Fishery	T-41-C
	*Family * wife: Katsuyo			
HAMAJI, Fujishirou (48)	Aza Shibaguchi, Kagami-cho, Yashiro-gun, Kumamoto	Lima, Peru, South America	Restaurant	V-27
	*Family * wife: Miyoshi; first son: Takashi; first daughter: Emiko			
HAMAMOTO, Kiichi (50)	Edajima-mura, Aki-gun, Hiroshima Pref.	Seattle, Washington	Railroad worker	Q-38-3
	*Family * wife: Chiyoko			

(continued)

CRYSTAL CITY REGISTRY JAPANESE FAMILY LIST February 11 1945 *(continued)*

Name (Age)	Primary Address	Previous Address	Occupation	Section No.
HARADA, Masakazu (66)	Kawaguchi-mura, Houtaku-gun, Kumamoto Pref.	Pismo Beach, California	Teacher	EQ-93-4
	*Family * wife: Megumi; first son: Higo			
HASEGAWA, Jiro(57)	Kameido-cho, Koto-ku, Tokyo	Lima, Peru, South California	Industry	DV-92-A
	*Family * none			
HASHIMOTO, Kinzou (65)	Urakami-mura, Higashimui-gun, Wakayama Pref.	Redwood, California	N/A	T-58-B
	*Family * wife: Mata			
HASHIMOTO, Kan (29)	Kuroki-cho, Yame-gun, Fukuoka	Lima, Peru, South America	Accountancy	Q-58-2
	*Family * wife: Setsuko			
HASHIMOTO, Saichi (54)	Ohkuma-mura, Tamura-gun, Fukushima Pref.	Torjillo, Peru, South America	Dentist	T-48-B
	*Family * wife: Omon; second son: Sasuke; third son: Satoshi; fifth daughter: Mitsuko			
HATANAKA, Yoshisuke (55)	Maehara-cho, Itoshima-gun, Fukuoka Pref.	Brawley, California	Agriculture	Q-57-1
	*Family * wife: Hanako; first son: Yoshimi; second son: Shigeo; third son: Hironobu; first daughter: Hanano			

HATTA, Masayoshi (38)	Kuroki-cho, Yame-gun, Fukuoka Pref.	Visco, Peru, South America	Restaurant	T-22-BC
	*Family * wife: Tamaki; first son: Masaharu; first daughter: Harumi; second daughter: Masako; third daughter: Hiromi			
HAYAKAWA, Kazumasa (42)	Tsunoda-mura, Chikujo-gun, Fukuoka Pref.	Hawthorne, California	Greenhouse	D-28-A
	*Family * wife: Takako, first daughter: Kimiyo, second daughter: Chiyoko; third daughter: Shinobu; fourth daughter: Itsuko			
HAYAMA, Hisao (43)	Tsunoda-mura, Chikujo-gun, Fukuoka Pref.	Kaniete, Peru, South America	Material shop	V-65
	*Family * wife: Yuri; first son: Hisato; first daughter: Toshiko			
HAYASHI, Kishirou (26)	Takatoki-mura, Ika-gun, Shiga Pref.	Lima, Peru, South America	Business	Q-64-2
	*Family * wife: Yukie; first son: Tomoki			
HAYASHIDA, Toriyoshi (47)	Ueki-cho, Shikamoto-gun, Kumamoto Pref.	Chiclayo, Peru, South America	Café	Q-63-2
	*Family * wife: Aiko; first son: Tetsuaki; second son: Tsukasa; first daughter: Masumi			
HIBINO, Yusaku (48)	Okamoto-mura, Ashiegami-gun, Kanagawa Pref.	San Francisco, California	Househusband	DV-131-A
	*Family * wife: Yoshie			

(*continued*)

CRYSTAL CITY REGISTRY JAPANESE FAMILY LIST February 11 1945 *(continued)*

Name (Age)	Primary Address	Previous Address	Occupation	Section No.
HIDEJIMA, Rikimatsu (46)	Yasu-mura, Asakura-gun, Fukuoka Pref.	Seattle, Washington	Priest of Kinko-kyo	Q-53-1
	*Family * wife: Mumeo; first son: Toru; second son : Akira; first daughter: Michiko			
HIGA, Motoyasu (39)	Nago-cho, Kokutou-gun, Okinawa Pref.	Lima, Peru, South America	Business	T-9-ABC
	*Family * wife: Yasu; first son: Ryuya; second son: Tatsuya; third son: Kazuya; fourth son: Hiroya; fifth son: Haruya; first daughter: Neri, second daughter: Yoshino; third daughter: Satsuki			
HIGA, Keiji (41)	Nago-cho, Kokutou-gun, Okinawa Pref.	Lima, Peru, South America	Barber	Q-69-4
	*Family * wife: Shizue; first daughter: Noriko			
HIGA, Kensuke (55)	Nago-cho, Kokutou-gun, Okinawa Pref.	Kaiyao, Peru, South America	Brewery	EQ-91-3
	*Family * wife: Kamado; first son: Kenyu; fifth son: Kenma; fourth daughter: Tomiko; fifth daughter: Yoshie			
HIGASHI, Toyokichi (51)	Shikine-mura, Shira-gun, Kagoshima Pref.	Inglewood, California	Agriculture	D-8-A
	*Family * wife: Chie, first son: Toyohisa; second son: Mitsuru; first daughter: Toshiko; second daughter: Yukiko			

HIGASHIDA, Haruo (57)	Tanbaichi-cho, Yamanabe-gun, Nara Pref.	Los Angeles, California	Missionary	D-20-B
	*Family * wife: Naka; second son: Kunio; third son: Sumio; third daughter: Kuniko; fourth daughter: Haruka			
HIGASHIDE, Seiichi (36)	Otoe-mura, Kuchi-gun, Hokkaido	Ica, Peru, South America	Business	T-25-AC
	*Family * wife: Shizuka; first son: Shuichi; second son: Hideki; first daughter: Sachiko; second daughter: Setsuko; third daughter: Maruta			
HIRAMINE, Takeji (34)	Eimei-mura, Yushuku-gun, Kagoshima Pref.	Lima, Peru, South America	Bakery	T-20-A
	*Family * wife: Nobu; first son: Akira; first daughter: Etsuko			
HIRANO, Kuro (50)	Mitsu-mura, Kamo-gun, Hiroshima Pref.	Wankaiyo, Peru, South America	Restaurant	T-3-B
	*Family * wife: Kawayo; grandson: HIRANO, Kiyoto			
HIRASHIMA, Matatarou (70)	Hisakatsu-mura, Awa-gun, Tokushima Pref.	Seattle, Washington	Missionary	D-11-B
	*Family * wife: Tatsu			
HIRAYAMA, Masashizu (43)	Yasu-mura, Asakura-gun, Fukuoka Pref.	Kauai, Hawaii	Missionary	D-49-A
	*Family * wife: Shige; first son: Mitsuo, second son: Masae; third son: Yukio; first daughter: Kyoko			

(*continued*)

CRYSTAL CITY REGISTRY JAPANESE FAMILY LIST February 11 1945 *(continued)*

Name (Age)	Primary Address	Previous Address	Occupation	Section No.
HIROKANE, Chouta (49)	Akinaka-mura, Kuga-gun, Yamaguchi Pref.	Clarksburg, California	Agriculture	V-119
	*Family * wife: Takiko; first son: Takashi; second son: Kota; third son: Hirota; first daughter: Mariko; second daughter: Sachiko; third daughter: Ruriko; fourth daughter: Fukuko			
HIROTSU, Kikunoshin (56)	Hirao-cho, Kumige-gun, Yamaguchi Pref.	Walnut Grove, California	Business	Q-55-1
	*Family * wife: Ichi; second son: Sei; third son: Jun			
HONDA, Eisaku (63)	Migoku-mura, Shikamoto-gun, Kumamoto Pref.	Honolulu, Hawaii	Teacher	T-56-C
	*Family * wife: Hatsumo			
HONDA, Masaki (42)	Wakajima-mura, Yashiro-gun, Kumamoto Pref.	Lima, Peru, South America	Poultry farming	D-22-A
	*Family * wife: Fujie; first son: Yoshinari; second son: Takashi; third son: Hiroshi; fourth son: Chikara; first daughter: Naoko			
HONDA, Mineki (45)	Kagami-cho, Yashiro-gun, Kumamoto Pref.	Delano, California	Business	D-6-B
	*Family * wife: Shigeno; first son: Shigeto; fourth son: Setsuo; first daughter: Chieko			

HOUJYOU, Nichizo (57)	Misaki-cho, Kanda-ku, Tokyo	Portland, Oregon	Food store	T-44-B
	*Family * wife: Yukiyo			
HORI, Heishiki (57)	Komakoshi-cho, Shimizu-city, Shizuoka Pref.	Lima, Peru, South America	Watchmaker	Q-68-3
	*Family * wife: Etsuko			
HORI, Isaburo (60)	Komakoshi-cho, Shimizu-city, Shizuoka Pref.	San Pedro, California	Fishery	D-21-B
	*Family * wife: Kin; first daughter: Hisayo; second daughter: Toshi; third daughter: Mitsue; fourth daughter: Yoshiko			
HORIBA, Kakutaro (45)	Arito-mura, Abe-gun, Shizuoka Pref.	Lima, Peru, South America	Agriculture	Q-66-2
	*Family * wife: Oei; first son: Kenichi; second son: Toru; third son: Tatsuya; fourth son: Katsu-toshi; fifth son: Nori; first daughter:Sumie			
HORIBE, Kiku (67)	Atago-mura, Kumage-gun, Yamaguchi Pref.	Kauai, Hawaii	Priest of Konko-kyo	T-42-C
	*Family * none			
HORIE, Sukesaburo (57)	Hikawa-mura, Yamada-gun, Gunma Pref.	Torrance, California	Agriculture	Q-41-1
	*Family * wife: Kame; first son: Kunio; first daughter: Sakiyo			

(continued)

CRYSTAL CITY REGISTRY JAPANESE FAMILY LIST February 11 1945 (*continued*)

Name (Age)	Primary Address	Previous Address	Occupation	Section No.
HOSHIJIMA, Kazuichi (43)	Toyokawa-mura, Tsukubo-gun, Okayama Pref.	Pasadena, California	Business	T-57-B
	*Family * wife: Chiyo; mother: HOSHIJIMA, Take			
HOSAKA, Souhichi (52)	Doshi-cho, Kaho-gun, Fukuoka Pref.	San Diego, California	Agriculture	Q-43-1
	*Family * wife: Misao; first son: Masato; second son: Masanori; first daughter: Ayako; second daughter: Sayoko			
HOSOKAWA, Masakado (63)	Ohama-cho, Hakata-city, Fukuoka Pref.	Kaiao, Peru, South America	Business	Q-68-1
	*Family * wife: Tomi			
HYODO, Masakazu (39)	Kinoe-cho, Toyoda-gun, Hiroshima Pref.	Santa Barbara, California	Business	T-61-C
	*Family * wife: Yoshie			
(I)				
ICHIBA, Isao (48)	Funakoshi-cho, Aki-gun, Hiroshima Pref.	Oahu, Hawaii	Teacher	T-45-C
	*Family * wife: Misao			

ICHIKAWA, Tatsuya (42)	Iiyama-mura, Shimo miuchi-gun, Nagano Pref.	Seattle, Washington	Missionary	Q-55-3
	*Family * wife: Yu; first son: Tatsu; second son: Kazuya; third son: Akira; fourth son: Nobuya; first daughter: Etsuko; second daughter: Noriko; third daughter: Hiroko			
IDENO, Jyunzo (43)	Takahama-cho, Matsuyama-city, Ehime Pref.	San Francisco, California	Business	D-22-B
	*Family * wife: Ayako; first son: Kazuo; second son: Shizuo			
IKEDA, Yoshizaemon (38)	Kuwaori-cho, Date-gun, Fukushima Pref.	Lima, Peru, South America	Material shop	Q-52-1
	*Family * wife: Kino; first son: Yoshiaki; second son: Hiroshi; third son: Susumu; fourth son: Isamu; first daughter: Kiyoko			
IKEDA, Soichi (33)	Kitakawa-mura, Oda-gun, Okayama Pref.	Wararu, Peru, South America	Brewery	EQ-77-1
	*Family * wife: Losa; first son: Kenichi; second son: Akio; third son: Nobuo; sister-in-law: MATSUKAWA, Tomiko			
IBARAHARA, Michimori (26)	Yamakawa-cho, Yushuku-gun, Kagoshima Pref.	Lima, Peru, South America	Clothing shop	D-43-A
	*Family * father: Ichisuke; mother: Kikue; brother: Hiroshi; sister: Sumiko			

(continued)

CRYSTAL CITY REGISTRY JAPANESE FAMILY LIST February 11 1945 *(continued)*

Name (Age)	Primary Address	Previous Address	Occupation	Section No.
IKEMIYA, Shigeaki (40)	Kitajima-cho, Wakayama-city, Wakayama Pref.	Alimert, California	Agriculture	D-13-B
	*Family * wife: Kitae; first son: Susumu; second son: Isao; first daughter: Michiyo			
IKENAGA, Yaebei (49)	Utsuga-mura, Otsu-gun, Yamaguchi Pref.	Hauha, Peru, Suth America	Material shop	T-14-BC
	*Family * wife: Yukino; fourth son: Mitsuro; fifth son: Youhachi; sixth son: Tadaaki; second daughter: Sumiko			
IKEGAMI, Kaneyoshi (56)	Makurazaki-cho, Kawabe-gun, Kagoshima Pref.	Porterville, California	Agriculture	D-51-A
	*Family * second son: Toshihide; first daughter: Nobuko; second daughter: Yoshiko			
IMAKITA, Rikizo (50)	Naruo-mura, Nishinomiya-city, Hyogo Pref.	Marshall Island	Agriculture	V-6-O
	*Family * wife: Etsuko			
IMAMURA, Shigenobu (54)	Kawai-cho, Yokkaichi-city, Mie Pref.	San Diego, California	Business	Q-39-3
	*Family * wife: Nao; second daughter: Sumiko; third daughter: Hisako; fourth daughter: Toshiko			

IMAMURA, Yasujiro (45)	Esumi-mura, Nishimui-gun, Wakayama Pref.	Guadalupe, California	Agriculture	D-35-B
	*Family * wife: Tokuko; first son: Tatsumi; second son: Eiji; first daughter: Sachiko; second daughter: Akiko; third daughter: Sadako			
INABA, Oyayasu (43)	Yutaka-mura, Chikuba-gun, Ibaragi Pref.	Riverside, California	Poultry farming	T-50-A
	*Family * wife: Kiri; first son: Akira; second son: Mitsuru; third son: Shizuo; first daughter: Midori; second daughter: Haru; third daughter: Setsu; fourth daughter: Hanako			
INABA, Hideo (41)	Yutaka-mura, Chikuba-gun, Ibaragi Pref.	Riverside, California	Dentist	D-39-B
	*Family * wife: Chiyo; first son: Hideo; second son: Isamu; third son: Takeshi			
INAGAKI, Kumekichi (50)	Tado-mura, Kuwana-gun, Mie Pref.	Lima, Peru, South America	Bakery	EQ-77-3
	*Family * wife: Setsu; first son: Kazuo; third son: Tomio; fourth son:Tsuneo; fifth son: Fumitaka			
INAKI, Toyojiro (47)	Sanjyo-cho, Hiroshima-city, Hiroshima Pref.	Fresno, California	Machinery	D-26-A
	*Family * wife: Toyoko; first son: Mikiro; first daughter: Noriyo; second daughter: Fusako			

(*continued*)

CRYSTAL CITY REGISTRY JAPANESE FAMILY LIST February 11 1945 *(continued)*

Name (Age)	Primary Address	Previous Address	Occupation	Section No.
INAYOSHI, Junichi (47)	Yumisaku-mura, Mitsui-gun, Fukuoka Pref.	Kaiyao, Peru, South America	Hardware seller	Q-61-2
	*Family * wife: Kimie; third son: Jun; first daughter: Michie			
INOGUCHI, Nushio (51)	Furukawa-mura, Yame-gun, Fukuoka Pref.	Lima, Peru, South America	Bakery	EQ-92-4
	*Family * wife: Tsuya; seventh daughter: Tamaki			
INOUE, Hisao (36)	Fucyu-cho, Ashishina-gun, Hiroshima Pref.	San Francisco, California	Merchant	D-40-A
	*Family * wife: Aiko; first son: Akio; second son: Tsuneo; mother: Kane			
INOUE, Susumu (41)	Aki-cho, Aki-gun, Kochi Pref.	Redwood, California	Flower gardener	T-58-A
	*Family * wife: Itsuyo; first daughter: Sachiko; second daughter: Junko; third daughter: Keiko			
ISHIDA, Hisakichi (63)	Sanjo-cho, Hiroshima-city, Hiroshima Pref.	Kaniete, Peru, South America	Business	V-7
	*Family * wife: Shite			
ISHIDA, Yasuhei (50)	Hon-machi, Sanjo-cho, Hiroshima-city, Hiroshima Pref.	Lima, Peru, South America	Material shop	V-8
	*Family * wife: Shizue; first son: Makoto; second son: Kenjiro; third son: Yasuo; first daughter: Ikue			

ISHIDA, Hiama (43)	Toriyama-cho, Setagaya-ku, Tokyo	San Francisco, California	Missionary	D-61-A
	*Family * wife: Chiyoko; first son: Hidemaro; second son: Kunimaro; third son:Kihimaro; first daughter: Taeko; second daughter: Noriko; third daughter: Hasuko; mother-in-law: SAITO, Hina			
ISHII, Yuzo (49)	Ino-mura, Kimitsu-gun, Chiba Pref.	Lima, Peru, South America	Clerk	Q-38-1
	*Family * wife: Toyo			
ISHIKAWA, Kiyoshi (49)	Shinoyama-cho, Taki-gun, Hyogo Pref.	Norfolk, California	Clergyman	Q-39-4
	*Family * wife: Tomoe; first daughter: Akiko			
ISHIYAMA, Torazo (54)	Funa-machi, Yotsuya-ku, Tokyo	Pasadena, California	Agriculture	Q-51-3
	*Family * wife: Miruko; first daughter: Haruko			
ISHIZAKI, Senmatsu (47)	Ozato-cho, Moji-city, Fukuoka Pref.	Carlsbad, California	Newspaper writer	EQ-82-4
	*Family * wife: Yuzuko; first son: Shiro; second son: Bungo			
ISHIZU, Kyogoro (55)	Akegi-cho, Atake-gun, Yamaguchi Pref.	Ica, Peru, South America	Business	V-76
	*Family * wife: Tomi; first daughter: Guadalupe			

(continued)

CRYSTAL CITY REGISTRY JAPANESE FAMILY LIST February 11 1945 *(continued)*

Name (Age)	Primary Address	Previous Address	Occupation	Section No.
ISHIZUKA, Kunisaburo (47)	Saori-mura, Kaibe-gun, Aichi Pref.	Walnut grove, California	Agriculture	T-31-A
	*Family * wife: Taka; second daughter: Kiyoko			
ISOBE, Hichinosuke (36)	Hane-mura, Aki-gun, Kochi Pref.	Redwood, California	Flower gardener	T-38-C
	*Family * wife: Fumiko			
ISONO, Tadayoshi (41)	Kawachi-mura, Houtaku-gun, Kumamoto Pref.	Torjillo, Peru, South America	Material shop	D-46-A
	*Family * wife: Shika; first son: Mitsuo; second son: Noboru			
ISONO, Tamotsu (31)	Kawachi-mura, Houtaku-gun, Kumamoto Pref.	Chiclayo, Peru, South America	Material shop	Q-63-3
	*Family * wife: Kiyoka; first son: Yasuo; second son: Masao; first daughter: Miyoko			
ITAKURA, Uichiro (42)	Ichinomiya-mura, Kawaki-gun, Mie Pref.	San Mateo, California	Gardener	T-31-C
	*Family * wife: Misae			
ITO, Kanzen (32)	Oguchi-mura, Tamba-gun, Aichi Pref.	Maui, Hawaii	Missionary	T-5-C
	*Family * none			

ITO, Kunimaro (42)	Tashiro-cho, Chigusa-ku, Nagoya-city, Aichi Pref.	Los Angeles, California	Missionary	D-39-A
	*Family * wife: Tamae; first son: Kunishige; second daughter: Yoshiko; third daughter: Fumiko; fourth daughter: Shizuko			
ITOKAZU, Tsunao (32)	Nishihara-mura, Chuto-gun, Okinawa Pref.	Lima, Peru, South America	Agriculture	T-15-BC
	*Family * wife: Kikue; first daughter: Misako; second daughter: Naoko; third daughter; Yasuko; father:Kozo			
IWAOKA, Masamitsu (49)	Kaito-mura, Masuki-gun, Kumamoto Pref.	Glendale, California	Business	T-60-C
	*Family * wife: Misae			
IWASAWA, Masaichi (56)	Jinho-cho, Hiroshima-city, Hiroshima Pref.	Delano, California	Barber	D-6-A
	*Family * wife: Kiyo; first son: Masami; second daughter: Shizuko; third daughter:Shigeko; fourth daughter: Kazuko			
IZUMI, Hikozo (32)	Yasu-mura, Asa-gun, Hiroshima Pref.	Chiclayo, Peru, South America	Merchant	Q-59-2
	*Family * wife: Masako; first son: Hisao			

(*continued*)

NAME (AGE)	PRIMARY ADDRESS	PREVIOUS ADDRESS	OCCUPATION	SECTION NO.
IZUMI, Kakusho (42)	Shikawa-mura, Kojo-gun, Saga Pref.	Papaloa, Hawaii	Missionary	D-57-A
	*Family * wife: Kiyo; first son: Takaaki; third son: Hiromichi; fourth son: Shin; second daughter: Junko; third daughter: Tomoko; fourth daughter: Norie; fifth daughter: Katsuyo			
(K)				
KAGE, Mantaro (56)	Shibakawa-mura, Uwa-gun, Fukuoka Pref.	Piula, Peru, South America	Business	DV-129
	*Family * wife: Michaela; first son: August; second son: Palsimon; third son: Julio; fourth son: Gielmo; first daughter: Francesca; second daughter: Neli; third daughter: Shizue; fourth daughter: Rosa			
KAGEYAMA, Yonetaro (55)	Kamohara-cho, Iorihara-gun, Shizuoka Pref.	Terminal Island, California	Fishery	T-33-C
	*Family * wife: Kin			
KAJIYA, Tokio (38)	Taniyama-cho, Kagoshima-gun, Kagoshima Pref.	Wacho, Peru, South America	Bakery	T-11-A
	*Family * wife: Yukie; first son: Hisashi; first daughter: Hiroko			
KAKUYA, Sansuke (51)	Komatsu-cho, Oshima-gun, Yamaguchi Pref.	Tacuna, Peru, South America	Material shop	V-38
	*Family * wife: Kiyoko; first son: Kazunari; first daughter: Kazumi; second daughter: Kazuyo			

KAMAYA, Toshihachi (43)	Nachi-cho, Higashimui-gun, Wakayama Pref.	Santa Ana, California	Agriculture	T-60-A
	*Family * wife: Yachiyo; first daughter: Toshiyo; second daughter: Yasuko; third daughter: Nobuko			
KANBE, Toshiharu (57)	Ono-mura, Kamiishi-gun, Hiroshima Pref.	Seattle, Washington	President of 'Nichibei Koron'	Q-38-2
	*Family * wife: Takako			
KAMIMURA, Hiroji (49)	Mase-cho, Kawabe-gun, Kagoshima Pref.	San Bernadino, California	Cleaning	DV-153-B
	*Family * wife: Taneko			
KAMISATO, Naohiko (49)	Izena-mura, Shimajiri-gun, Okinawa Pref.	Lima, Peru, South America	Bakery	Q-40-3
	*Family * wife: Ushi; second son: Yasuo; first daughter: Chieko; second daughter: Motoko			
KANEKAKI, Tatsuo (50)	Shirohata-mura, Masaki-gun, Kumamoto Pref.	Concord, California	Agriculture	D-50-A
	*Family * wife: Masame; first son: Akira; second son: Kiyoshi; first daughter: Hatsuko; second daughter: Taeko			
KANESHIRO, Tadahito (38)	Motobe-cho, Kokuto-gun, Okinawa Pref.	Lima, Peru, South America	Clerk	Q-65-2
	*Family * wife: Yoshie			

(*continued*)

CRYSTAL CITY REGISTRY JAPANESE FAMILY LIST February 11 1945 *(continued)*

Name (Age)	Primary Address	Previous Address	Occupation	Section No.
KANESHIRO, Kiyosaburo (33)	Makabe-mura, Shimajiri-gun, Okinawa Pref.	Lima, Peru, South America	Material shop	V-37
	*Family * wife: Mitsu; first daughter: Haruko; second daughter: Kinue			
KANEKO, Heitaro (48)	Torikawa-mura, Nobuo-gun, Fukushima Pref.	Seal Beach, California	Agriculture	Q-49-1
	*Family * wife: Mine; first son: Akira; second son: Masao; third son: Toshimoto; fourth son: Maroshi, first daughter: Kimie; second daughter: Mei; third daughter: Kinuyo			
KANEKO, Sumiaki (38)	Oya-mura, Iwase-gun, Fukushima Pref.	Lima, Peru, South America	Glass store	D-29-A
	*Family * wife: Otali; first son: Shoichi; second son: Shuji; first daughter: Momoko; third daughter: Noriyo			
KANEKO, Sumiyoshi (33)	Oya-mura, Iwase-gun, Fukushima Pref.	Lima, Peru, South America	Glass store	Q-38-4
	*Family * wife: Hikaru			
KANEKO, Yoshizo (47)	Hashimoto-cho, Kanda-ku, Tokyo	Lima, Peru, South America	Watchmaker	Q-63-1
	*Family * wife: Roku; first son: Fumiji; second son: Ken.			

KANOGAWA, Tadashi (53)	Mafutsu-mura, Naga-gun, Wakayama Pref.	Seattle, Washington	Food store	T-35-A
	*Family * wife: Shizu; first son: Shoji; second son: Akira; second daughter: Yaeko			
KASAI, Kenji (52)	Nishijima-mura, Minamishima-gun, Yamanashi Pref.	San Francisco, California	Bond company	D-26-B
	*Family * wife: Aya; first son: Shoichi; second son: Hideho			
KASHIWABARA, Tatsuhisa (33)	Fujio-mura, Ashina-gun, Hiroshima Pref.	Pabilo, Hawaii	Missionary	D-32-A
	*Family * wife: Kiyoko; first daughter: Keiko; third daughter: Yoko; fourth daughter: Yashio			
KATO, Tadahei (49)	Ukari-mura, Shuchi-gun, Shizuoka Pref.	Lima, Peru, South America	Business	DV-108
	*Family * wife: Noriko; first son: Tadahiko; second son: Tadaaki; first daughter: Fumiko; second daughter: Chieko; third daughter: Mieko; fourth daughter: Yoshiko; fifth daughter: Setsuko			
KATO, Magoichi (52)	Mie-mura, Nakashima-gun, Yamanashi Pref	Lima, Peru, South America	Liquor wholesaler	Q-65-4
	*Family * wife: Shizuko; second son: Kazumi; third son: Kazuo			
KATO, Shu (51)	Shin-machi, Setagaya-ku, Tokyo	Honolulu, Hawaii	Company director	V-47
	*Family * wife: Hideko, first son: Hiroshi			

(continued)

CRYSTAL CITY REGISTRY JAPANESE FAMILY LIST February 11 1945 *(continued)*

Name (Age)	Primary Address	Previous Address	Occupation	Section No.
KATSUTA, Tokushiro (58)	Mitsu-cho, Kamo-gun, Hiroshima Pref.	Wacho, Peru, South America	Tinplate seller	V-51
	*Family * first son: Harumi; first son's wife: Mitsue; grandson: Haruo; granddaughter: Chizuru, Mikiko			
KATSUNO, Asaichi (42)	Minomushi, Aoyama, Tokyo	Honolulu, Hawaii	Cook	DV-139-B
	*Family * wife: Hatsuyo; first son: Michio			
KAWABE, Sotaro (54)	Yonehara-cho, Sakata-gun, Shiga Pref.	Seward, Alaska	Business	T-19-B
	*Family * wife: Tomo			
KAWAGUCHI, Kikuzo (65)	Yasutake-mura, Minuma-gun, Fukuoka Pref.	Watsonville, California	Business	V-115
	*Family * wife: Kino; first son: Minato			
KAWAHARA, Seitaro (58)	Aikawa-mura, Mitsui-gun, Fukuoka Pref.	Calexico, California	Farming business	Q-42-2
	*Family * wife: Yae			

KAWAHIRA, Kiichi (40)	Eimei-mura, Yushuku-gun, Kagoshima Pref.	Sacramento, California	Agriculture	V-111
	*Family * wife: Yuko; first son: Masatomo; second son: Kenji; third son: Kenzo; fourth son: Isamu; fifth son: Susumu; first daughter: Tatsue; second daughter: Mutsuko			
KAWAI, Kingo (47)	Shimokawa-mura, Korigami-gun, Gifu Pref.	Visalia, California	Agriculture	V-36
	*Familly * wife: Riyo			
KAWAMOTO, Shigetaro (57)	Nanbu-cho, Hidaka-gun, Wakayama Pref.	Santa Maria, California	Agriculture	D-20-A
	*Family * wife: Yae; second son: Hiroshi			
KAWAMOTO, Ryuzo (38)	Fuchu-cho, Aki-gun, Hiroshima Pref.	Anaheim, California	Agriculture	D-5-A
	*Family * wife: Kazuko; first son: Noboru; second son: Kanichi; first daughter: Mieko; second daughter: Yukie			
KAWAMURA, Terumichi (39)	Kamihata-mura, Kuga-gun, Yamaguchi Pref.	Maui, Hawaii	Missionary	DV-140-A
	*Family * wife: Masako; first son: Hiromichi; second son: Hirotoshi			
KAWANO, Sadakichi (44)	Higashiyama-mura, Yamakado-gun, Fukuoka Pref.	Torjillo, Peru, South America	Business	T-56-B
	*Family * wife: Fuki; first son: Hiromichi			

(*continued*)

CRYSTAL CITY REGISTRY JAPANESE FAMILY LIST February 11 1945 *(continued)*

Name (Age)	Primary Address	Previous Address	Occupation	Section No.
KAWASAKI, Ryosaku (54)	Kariogawa-mura, Asa-gun, Hiroshima Pref.	Oahu, Hawaii	Carpenter	T-43-C
	*Family * wife: Miyuki			
KAWASHIMA, Noboru (39)	Akiyama-mura, Gokawa-gun, Kochi Pref.	Woodland, California	Agriculture	D-10-A
	*Family * wife: Toshiko; first son: Akio; second son: Toshiyuki; first daughter: Hisako; second daughter: Eiko; third daughter: Yoshiko			
KAWASHIMA, Tominosuke (47)	Kashiwagi-mura, Koga-gun, Shiga Pref.	Los Angeles, California	Business	EQ-81-3
	*Family * wife: Fumiyo; first son: Takashi; second son: Masao; first daughter: Mikako			
KAWADA, Takeshi (41)	Ukato-mura, Mitsu-gun, Okayama Pref.	Delano, California	Agriculture	T-61-B
	*Family * wife: Kuri; first daughter: Reiko			
KENMOCHI, Yasuo (41)	Arito-mura, Abe-gun, Shizuoka Pref.	Los Angeles, California	Fishery	EQ-80-1
	*Family * wife: Mieko; first daughter: Miyo			

KIDO, Masazo (57)	Arao-cho, Tamana-gun, Kumamoto Pref.	El Monte, California	Agriculture	D-54-B
	*Family * wife: Mitsu; second son: Yoshito; first daughter: Miyoko			
KIJIMA, Keiji (46)	Jyuni-cho, Shishuku-city, Kagoshima Pref.	New York city, New York	Dental technician	DV-95-A
	*Family * wife: Yuki			
KIMURA, Akio (45)	Waki-mura, Kuga-gun, Yamaguchi Pref.	Honolulu, Hawaii	Doctor	T-52-B
	*Family * none			
KIMURA, Shuji (64)	Takeo-cho, Nanjo-gun, Fukui Pref.	Hawaii Island, Hawaii	Teacher	Q-62-4
	*Family * wife: Hatsu			
KINO, Yasutada (33)	Nago-cho, Kokuto-gun, Okinawa Pref.	Piura, Peru, South America	Business	DV-96-A
	*Family * wife: Suma; father-in-law: TAKAMURA, Kaichiro			
KISHIMOTO, Kensho (35)	Nago-cho, Kokuto-gun, Okinawa Pref.	Lima, Peru, South America	Milk plant	EQ-91-1
	*Family * wife: Tsuruko; first son: Norihiro; second son: Hirofumi; third son: Hiroji; first daughter: Hideko; second daughter: Fusako			

(*continued*)

CRYSTAL CITY REGISTRY JAPANESE FAMILY LIST February 11 1945 *(continued)*

Name (Age)	Primary Address	Previous Address	Occupation	Section No.
KITAJIMA, Sadazo (45)	Yamakado-mura, Yamato-gun, Fukuoka Pref.	Piura, Peru, South America	Material shop	DV-124
	*Family * wife: Haruko; first son: Makoto; first daughter: Kazue; second daughter: Konami; third daughter: Michie			
KITTANI, Shosuke (41)	Shimookamura-cho, Bofu-city, Yamaguchi Pref.	Lima, Peru, South America	Business	D-43-B
	*Family * wife: Fumiko; first son: Takashi; second son: Hiroshi; third son: Kazumichi			
KIYAMA, Soshiro (60)	Ono-mura, Mitsu-gun, Okayama Pref.	Los Angeles, California	Farming business	DV-93-B
	*Family * wife: Chika; first daughter: Chieko; nephew: MUMODA, Satoru			
KOBAYASHI, Makio (41)	Toshiki-mura, Toshiki-gun, Fukui Pref.	Ogden, Utah	Cleaning	T-58-C
	*Family * wife: Onoyo			
KOBAYASHI, Masaichi (56)	Yashiro-mura, Oshima-gun, Yamaguchi Pref.	Honolulu, Hawaii	Business	DV-153-A
	*Family * wife: Chikayo			

KODAMA, Senpei (42)	Minamiyasuki-mura, Higashikokuto-gun, Oita Pref.	San Francisco, California	Mechanic	DV-134-B
	*Family * wife: Sueko			
KODAMA, Setsuji (59)	Jinho-cho, Hiroshima-city, Hiroshima Pref.	Monterey, California	Cleaning	D-1-A
	*Family * wife: Fujiko; first son: Jyoji; second son: Mitsuru; first daughter: Kiku; second daughter: Taeko			
KOGA, Takeshi (41)	Mikawa-mura, Miyoki-gun, Saga Pref.	San Francisco, California	Confectioner	D-7-A
	*Family * wife: Tomono; first son: Shoji; first daughter: Tomomi; second daughter: Kunie			
KONATSU, Takamasa (38)	Tamaki-mura, Shimajiri-gun, Okinawa Pref.	Lima, Peru, South America	Business	T-10-A
	*Family * wife: Kiyo; first son: Masaru; second son: Yuzuru; first daughter: Keiko			
KOIKE, Shiyoshi (60)	Kuboizumi-mura, Saga-gun, Saga Pref.	Hortville (sic), California	Agriculture	T-34-A
	*Family * wife: Teru; first son: Ryoichi; second son: Teruo			
KOIZUMI, Shigejiro (37)	Goki-cho, Nakano, Honjo-ku, Tokyo	Chanchamayo, Peru, South America	Agriculture	DV-92-B
	*Family * wife: Hiroko, first daughter: Yoko, second daughter: Akiko			

(*continued*)

CRYSTAL CITY REGISTRY JAPANESE FAMILY LIST February 11 1945 *(continued)*

Name (Age)	Primary Address	Previous Address	Occupation	Section No.
KOJIMA, Kazuo (43)	Kijima-cho, Arita-gun, Wakayama Pref.	Los Angeles, California	Business	T-37-A
	*Family * wife: Koyuki; first son: Satoshi; first daughter: Sachiko			
KOJIMA, Sadakichi (55)	Morimoto-cho, Azabu-ku, Tokyo	Honolulu, Hawaii	Book store	T-62-C
	*Family * first daughter: Mari			
KOUKETSU, Kumao (49)	Meikawa-mura, Ena-gun, Gifu Pref.	Brawley, California	Agriculture	Q-57-4
	*Family * wife: Sachiko; first son: Masao; first daughter: Junko; second daughter: Ayako			
KAWANO, Isamu (49)	Kasaoki-mura, Higashiuwa-gun, Ehime Pref.	Torrance, California	Aguriculture	Q-51-4
	*Family * first son: Hiroshi			
OYAMA, Takaya (41)	Toyooka-mura, Minamishima-gun, Yamanashi Pref.	Lima, Peru, South America	Business	Q-40-4
	*Family * wife: Takeyo; first son: Michio; second son: Masamizu			
KUBO, Yoshita	Katsume-mura, Kawabe-gun, Kagoshima Pref.	San Diego, California	Cleaning	D-25-B
	*Family * wife: Tsuru; first son: Yoshiaki; second son: Teruo			

KUBOTA, Yoshio (39)	Kamohara-cho, Iorihara-gun, Shizuoka Pref.	Terminal Island, California	Fishery	EQ-82-1
	*Family * wife: Hiroko; first son: Yoshihiro			
KUBO, Hidemaro (43)	Hon-machi, Niinomiya-city, Wakayama Pref.	Brawley, California	Farming business broker	T-32-B
	*Family * wife: Masako; first son: Hide			
KUBO, Yoshifumi (68)	Hon-machi, Niinomiya-city, Wakayama Pref.	Brawley, California	N/A	Q-62-2
	*Family * wife: Sai			
KUDAKA, Shuei (43)	Yotaniyama-mura, Chuto-gun, Okinawa Pref.	Kaiyao, Peru, South America	Restaurant	EQ-83-3
	*Family * wife: Tsuru			
KUDO, Rokuichi (52)	Isoko-cho, Yokohama-city, Kanagawa Pref.	Lima, Peru South America	Import business	EQ-85-1
	*Family * wife: Yoshiko; fourth son: Shiro; fifth son: Eigo; first daughter: Nami			
KUDO, Hirotsune (52)	Iwato-mura, Nishiusuki-gun, Miyazaki Pref.	Lima, Peru, South America	Hotel	DV-131-B
	*Family * wife: Shigemi; first son: Yuhiro; first daughter: Shizuko; second daughter: Kiyoko			

(*continued*)

CRYSTAL CITY REGISTRY JAPANESE FAMILY LIST February 11 1945 *(continued)*

Name (Age)	Primary Address	Previous Address	Occupation	Section No.
KUGA, Naoyoshi (41)	Yasu-mura, Asakura-gun, Fukuoka Pref.	Alameda, California	Gardener	Q-40-1
	*Family * wife: Aiko; first son: Masayoshi; first daughter: Chitose			
KUMAMOTO, Yoshinori (47)	Yanai-cho, Kuga-gun, Yamaguchi Pref.	Los Angeles, California	Farming business	Q-70-4
	*Family * wife: Tatsuko; third son: Tsutomu; second daughter: Katsue			
KURAKANE, Tsune (46)	Obama-cho, Adachi-gun, Fukushima Pref.	Los Angeles, California	Gardener	Q-52-3
	*Family * wife: Haruyo; first son: Shoichi; first daughter: Miruko; second daughter: Kiyoko; third daughter: Yoshiko			
KURATA, Yoshitaro (54)	Aso-mura, Kibi-gun, Okayama Pref.	Gardena, California	Business	EQ-94-3
	*Family * wife: Misao			
KURIKAWA, Motoichi (55)	Sugano-mura, Micho-gun, Hiroshima Pref.	Wacho, Peru, South America	Agriculture	EQ-83-3
	*Family * wife: Kimi; first son: Gen; first daughter: Yoshimi; second daughter: Kiyoko; adopted daughter: Sachiko			

KUSAKA, Kumataro (46)	Kushimoto-cho, Nishimui-gun, Wakayama Pref.	Terminal Island, California	Agriculture	T-52-B
	*Family * wife: Raku; first daughter: Keiko			
KUWAHARA, Tsunematsu (47)	Teno-mura, Amakusa-gun, Kumamoto Pref.	Pescadero, California	Agriculture	T-23-A
	*Family * wife: Yuku; second son: Isamu; first daughter: Hatsue; third daughter: Michie			
KUMA, Hanjiro (51)	Yokoyama-mura, Yame-gun, Fukuoka Pref.	Lima, Peru, South America	Poultry farming	Q-60-2
	*Family * wife: Yayoi; first son: Tatsuo; first daughter: Sakae; second daughter: Sumie; third daughter: Tsutae; mother-in-law: HISAKAWA, Mitsune			
(M)				
MAEKAWA, Kazuo (33)	Kitami-mura, Shikamoto-gun, Kumamoto Pref.	Balanco, Peru, South America	Watchmaker	T-14-A
	*Family * wife: Hatsu; first daughter: Junko; second daughter: Noriko			
MAEOKA, Sakutaro (52)	Kawachi-mura, Futami-gun, Hiroshima Pref.	Torjillo, Peru, South America	Carpenter	V-11-12
	*Family * wife: Sekino; first son: Kenji; second son: Juro; third son: Tetsuo; first daughter: Akiko; second daughter: Mayuko			

(*continued*)

CRYSTAL CITY REGISTRY JAPANESE FAMILY LIST February 11 1945 *(continued)*

Name (Age)	Primary Address	Previous Address	Occupation	Section No.
MAESHIBA, Naojiro (33)	Kushimoto-cho, Nishimui-gun, Wakayama Pref.	San Diego, California	Fishery	Q-50-4
	*Family * wife: Misae; first son: Naoki; first daughter: Shigeno			
MAKIMOTO, Kiyoto	Inoguchi-mura, Saeki-gun, Hiroshima Pref.	Visco, Peru, South America	Restaurant	V-13
	*Family * Ayako; first son: Haruo; second son: Nobuyuki; first daughter: Asako; second daughter: Sumiko; third daughter: Tamee; fourth daughter: Akemi			
MAKINO, Hiroshi (52)	Tawara-mura, Shikamoto-gun, Kumamoto Pref.	Guadalupe, California	Agriculture	D-44-B
	*Family * wife: Komitsu; first son: Koichi; first daughter: Hiroko; second daughter: Michiko			
MAMIYA, Toshio (36)	Nakano-mura, Kamou-gun, Shiga Pref.	Hacaula (sic), Hawaii	Missionary	T-39-B
	*Family * wife: Teruko; first son: Teruo; second son: Akio			
MANAKI, Usaburo (51)	Wakiyama-mura, Sagara-gun, Fukuoka Pref.	Chiclayo, Peru, South America	Business	D-34-B
	*Family * wife: Hitomi; first son: Mitsuo; first daughter: Sadako; second daughter: Hideko			

[illegible]	[illegible] Fukuoka Pref.	Chiclayo, Peru, South America	Business	Q-65-3
	*Family * wife: Haruyo			
MARUI, Youemon (44)	Sapei-cho, Nishikowa-gun, Ehime Pref.	Watsonville, California	Farming business	D-18-A
	*Family * wife: Haruko; first son: Hiroshi; first daughter: Tsuneko			
MASACHIKA, Tochiichi (50)	Kanme-mura, Kume-gun, Okayama Pref.	Lima, Peru, South America	Barber	EQ-75-1
	*Family * wife: Yoshito			
MASAKI, Kengo (35)	Mihara-mura, Tomochi-gun, Shimane Pref.	Kaiyao, Peru, South America	Milk plant	EQ-76-1
	*Family * wife: Hideko; first son: Hiroshi; second son: Takashi; first daughter: Nobeko; second daughter: Tomoko; third daughter: Takako; fourth daughter: Mineko			
MASUDA, Taro (39)	Hiura-mura, Asa-gun, Hiroshima Pref.	Lodi, California	Agriculture	Q-44-1
	*Family * wife: Chiyomi; first son: Tokio; first daughter: Emiko; second daughter: Moshiko; third daughter: Sushiko; fourth daughter: Ruriko; brother: Mikio			
MATOBA, Mineo (49)	Rokui-mura, Asa-gun, Hiroshima Pref.	Santa Maria, California	Business	D-55-A
	*Family * wife: Yoshio; first son: Hideomi; first daughter: Hatsumi; second daughter: Tomiko			

(*continued*)

CRYSTAL CITY REGISTRY JAPANESE FAMILY LIST February 11 1945 *(continued)*

Name (Age)	Primary Address	Previous Address	Occupation	Section No.
MATSUBAYASHI, Moriichi (33)	Misumi-cho, Otsu-gun, Yamaguchi Pref.	Lima, Peru, South America	Car manufacturer	Q-70-1
	*Family * wife: Atsuko; first son: Kazuo; second son: Akio; third son: Tetsuo			
MATSUBAYASHI, Shigezo (50)	Kawara-machi, Hagi-city, Yamaguchi Pref.	Lima, Peru, South America	Car manufacturer	EQ-76-3
	*Family * wife: Natsuko; first son: Isao; second son: Toshio; third son: Tadao; first daughter: Michie; second daughter: Kimiko; third daughter: Akemi; fourth daughter: Shigeko			
MATSUDA, Kunikichi (42)	Kawabe-cho, Kawabe-gun, Kagoshima Pref.	Lima, Peru, South America	Agriculture	EQ-78-1
	*Family * wife: Hisako; first son: Seiichi; second son: Sakuro; first daughter: Sumiko; second daughter: Kyoko; third daughter: Ayako			
MATUDA, Yanaharu (56)	Yotaniyama-mura, Chuto-gun, Okinawa Pref	Wararu, Peru, South America	Agriculture	V-62
	*Family * wife: Nabe; first daughter: Shizuko			
MATSUDO, Rokusuke (50)	Hachiman-mura, Higashiyamanashi-gun, Yamanashi Pref	Los Angeles, California	Business	D-40-A
	*Family * wife: Nagako;; first son: Wataru; second son: Sei			

MATSUI, Totayoshi (51)	Sakumoto-mura, Shiga-gun, Shiga Pref.	Honolulu, Hawaii	Bank	T-24-A
	*Family * wife: Tatsuko; first daughter: Nobuko; nephew: Yoshikazu			
MATSUMOTO, Kazuichi (61)	Mino-mura, Fukayasu-gun, Hiroshima Pref	Petaluma, California	Poultry farming	D-27-B
	*Family * wife: Chika; first son: Kazumi; first daughter: Midori; second daughter: Fusae			
MATSUSHIMA, Umata (45)	Hiratsu-mura, Mitsu-gun, Okayama Pref.	Portland, Oregon	Trade business	T-59-A
	*Family * wife: Fumi; second son: Yoji; third son: Hiroshi			
MATSUURA, Saburo (32)	Isoko-cho, Yokohama-city, Kanagawa Pref.	Lima, Peru, South America	Business	D-27-A
	*Family * wife: Kiyoko; first son: Yoshihiko; first daughter: Atsuko; second daughter: Kuniko			
MAEDA, Takahisa (40)	Idemizu-cho, Kumamoto-city, Kumamoto Pref.	Molokai, Hawaii	Teacher	T-16-A
	*Family * wife: Haruko; first daughter: Tomoko; second daughter: Kinko			
MIKAMI, Nobuo (55)	Miharucho, Tamura-gun, Fukushima Pref.	Brentwood, California	Agriculture	T-5-B
	*Family * wife: Sen			

(continued)

CRYSTAL CITY REGISTRY JAPANESE FAMILY LIST February 11 1945 (*continued*)

NAME (AGE)	PRIMARY ADDRESS	PREVIOUS ADDRESS	OCCUPATION	SECTION NO.
MIKUNI, Kensaku (52)	Shimono-mura, Kamo-gun, Hiroshima Pref.	Wararu, Peru, South America	Agriculture	V-70
	*Family * wife: Lise; second son: Toyoji; third son: Kenji			
MINAMI, Shinichi (42)	Bame-mura, Hidaka-gun, Wakayama Pref.	Ensenada, Mexico	Fishery	D-15-B
	*Family * wife: Shizuko; second son: Katsuji; first daughter: Eiko			
MISHIMA, Shoichi (47)	Kamo-mura, Fukayasu-gun, Hiroshima Pref.	Lima, Peru, South America	Haberdashery	EQ-72-1
	*Family * wife: Kikuno; first son: Susumu; first daughter: Yuriko; second daughter: Miyoko			
MISHIMA, Tasaku (40)	Nadasaki-mura, Kojima-gun, Okayama Pref.	Kaniete, Peru, South America	Material shop	V-3132
	*Family * wife: Shizuka; first son: Noboru; second son: Kazunari; third son: Masaru; first daughter: Masako			
MIHASHI, Kensuki (42)	Fukuzawa-mura, Ashiegami-gun, Kanagawa Pref.	Guadalupe, California	Mechanic	T-40-B
	*Family * wife: Ura; first daughter: Kazae			

MIYAHIRA, Kozo (54)	Hanechi-mura, Kokuto-gun, Okinawa Pref.	Kaiyao, Peru, South America	Noodle plant	EQ-75-3
	*Family *wife: Sumiko; first son: Tetsuo; second son: Tadashige; third son: Tadanobu; first daughter: Setsuko; second daughter: Emiko			
MIYAMOTO, Fumitetsu (56)	Hisami-cho, Kaibe-gun, Oita Pref.	Oahu, Hawaii	Missionary	D-59-A
	*Family * wife: Fumi; third son: Terufumi; first daughter: Taeko; second daughter: Keiko			
MIYAOU, Shigemaru (41)	Mineda-mura, Hiba-gun, Hiroshima Pref.	Honolulu, Hawaii	Missionary of Shinto	T-36-A
	*Family * wife: Yuki; second son: Takaomi; third son: Masanori; first daughter: Junko			
MIYAOU, Yoshie (53)	Kuchiwa-mura, Tomochi-gun, Shimane Pref.	Honolulu, Hawaii	Shinto Priest	T-52-C
	*Family * adopted daughter: MIKAMI, Atsuko			
MIYOSHI, Shinkichi (67)	Dote-cho, Hiroshima-city, Hiroshima Pref.	Terminal Island, California	Shinto Priest	D-2-A
	*Family * first daughter: Fumiko			
MIZUKAMI, Fumikichi (42)	Mimi-mura, Sanpo-gun, Fukui Pref.	Elk, California	Agriculture	T-29-A
	*Family * wife: Suma; first son: Kiyoshi; second son: Iwao			

(*continued*)

CRYSTAL CITY REGISTRY JAPANESE FAMILY LIST February 11 1945 *(continued)*

Name (Age)	Primary Address	Previous Address	Occupation	Section No.
MIZUTA, Noboru (46)	Nagataba-mura, Asa-gun, Hiroshima Pref.	Lima, Peru, South America	Fuel wholesaler	EQ-90-1
	*Family * wife: Yukiko; first son: Hirohide; second son: Hideo; first daughter: Kimie; second daughter: Reiko			
MONMA, Eisaburo (58)	Kori-cho, Kori-gun, Miyagi Pref.	Supe, Peru, South America	Agriculture	V-3
	*Family * wife: Kumayo			
MONMA, Tomio (35)	Kori-cho, Kori-gun, Miyagi Pref.	Supe, Peru, South America	Agriculture	V-4
	*Family * wife: Fuji; first son: Mitsuru; second son: Takashi; first daughter: Takako; second daughter: Miwako			
MORIYAMA, Souta (61)	Nagaito-mura, Itoshima-gun, Fukushima Pref.	Kaniete, Peru, South America	Material shop	DV-93-A
	*Family * wife: Hisano			
MORI, Motoichi (55)	Shinohara-mura, Enuma-gun, Ishikawa Pref.	Honolulu, Hawaii	Doctor	D-33-B
	*Family * wife: Ishiko			

MORIMOTO, Ichitaro (72)	Paliacoto, Lima, Peru, South America	Lima, Peru, South America	Business	T-32-C
	*Family * wife: Sachiko			
MORIMOTO, Toukichi (66)	Kagami-mura, Tosa-gun, Kochi Pref.	Hawthorne, Caifornia	Agriculture	D-35-A
	*Family * wife: Masaki; second son: Shiro			
MORIOKA, Tsuneshige (36)	Hirookagamino-mura, Gokawa-gun, Kochi Pref.	Marysville, California	Business	D-9-B
	*Family * wife: Kimiko; first son: Tomio; first daughter: Yuriko; second daughter: Chieko; third daughter: Sayoko			
MORISHIGE, Masatome (51)	Kamikunizaki-mura, Higashikokuto-gun, Oita Pref.	Torjillo, Peru, South America	Photo studio	V-5-6
	*Family * wife: Shizuka; first son: Yasushi; third daughter: Yoshiko; fourth daughter: Takako; fifth daughter: Tokuka; sixth daughter: Teruka			
MORITAKA, Suetaro (53)	Hemaki-mura, Kikuchi-gun, Kumamoto Pref.	Chiclayo, Peru, South America	Barber	D-32-B
	*Family * wife: Mitsue; first son: Nagato; first adughter: Nobuko; second daughter: Yoshiko; third daughter: Eiko, fourth daughter: Matsumi.			

(*continued*)

CRYSTAL CITY REGISTRY JAPANESE FAMILY LIST February 11 1945 *(continued)*

Name (Age)	Primary Address	Previous Address	Occupation	Section No.
MUKOYAMA, Koushiro (42)	Takau-cho, Nada-ku, Kobe-city, Hyogo Pref.	Lima, Peru, South America	Import business	D-16-B
	*Family * wife: Chiyoka, first son: Reiichiro, second son: Shojiro, third son: Takami, fourth son: Shigeru, first daughter: Misuzu			
MUNAKATA, Kurato (47)	Okumeda-mura, Aki-gun, Hiroshima Pref.	Chinchiya, Peru, South America	Haberdashery	V-78
	*Family * wife: Masako, first daughter: Reiko			
MURAKAMI, Kenji (40)	Moto-machi, Koriyama-city, Fukushima Pref.	Lima, Peru, South America	Import business	Q-71-3
	*Family * wife: Kimi, first son: Kazuo, second son: Norio, first daughter: Sachiko			
MURAKAMI, Samon (49)	Mamorikawa-mura, Kikuchi-gun, Kumamoto Pref.	Lima, Peru, South America	Carpenter	EQ-33-4
	*Family * wife: Motoe			
MURAKI, Sueo (36)	Utsuga-mura, Otsu-gun, Yamaguchi Pref.	Talma, Peru, South America	Haberdashery	T-13-A
	*Family * wife: Yasuko, first son: Hirokata, first daughter: Yoko			

MURAOKA, Saburo (44)	Okano-cho, Yokohama-city, Kanagawa Pref.	Chula Vista, California	Agriculture	T-48-A
	*Family * wife: Haruko; first son: Akitake; second son: Takenori; first daughter: Yoko; second daughter: Sadako			
MURATA, Yoichi (39)	Shimizu-mura, Nobuo-gun, Fukushima Pref.	Lima, Peru, South America	Fabric shop	Q-60-4
	*Family * wife: Yasuko; first son: Yoshiaki; second son: Hideki; mother: Nayo			
MURONO, Ginzo (35)	Amino-cho, Takeno-gun, Kyoto-fu	Lima, Peru, South America	Stationery shop	D-4-B
	*Family * wife: Hisayo; second son: Eisuke; third son: Masatake; first daughter: Tomiko			
MUROI, Masaru (49)	Asahida-cho, Minamikaizu-gun, Fukushima Pref.	Lima, Peru, South America	Cleaning	EQ-88-3
	*Family * wife: Hoshino			
MUTA, Kanji (30)	Yamamoto-mura, Mitsui-gun, Fukuoka Pref.	Chiclayo, Peru, South America	Shop clerk	T-45-B
	*Family * wife: Tomeko; first son: Kazuo; second son: Tomio			
MUTA, Mongo (34)	Yamamoto-mura, Mitsui-gun, Fukuoka Pref.	Chiclayo, Peru, South America	Glass store	D-46-B
	*Family * wife: Matsue; first son: Kunio; first daughter: Aiko; second daughter: Chieko			

(*continued*)

CRYSTAL CITY REGISTRY JAPANESE FAMILY LIST February 11 1945 *(continued)*

Name (Age)	Primary Address	Previous Address	Occupation	Section No.
MUTOBE, Tatsunori (42)	Takeu-cho, Nanjo-gun, Fukui Pref.	Oahu, Hawaii	Missionary	T-7-AB
	*Family * wife: Chiyoko; first son: Hironori; second son: Sadanori; third son: Masanori; fourth son Momonori; first daughter: Reiko; second daughter: Keiko; third daughter: Noriko			
(N)				
NADA, Yujiro (54)	Funakoshi-cho, Aki-gun, Hiroshima Pref.	Oahu, Hawaii	Teacher	D-45-A
	*Family * wife: Shigeyo; first son: Ichiro; second son: Jiro; first daughter: Kazuko; second daughter: Masako.			
NAGANUMA, Iwaichi (54)	Aikawa-mura, Chikujo-gun, Fukuoka Pref.	Kaiyao, Peru, South America	Cleaning	EQ-90-3
	*Family * wife: Isoka; first son: Kazuyoshi; third son: Kazunari; fourth son: Kazuaki; fifth son: Kazumichi; first daughter: Shizuka; second daughter: Kiyoka; third daughter: Sumika			
NAGAO, Morozou (38)	Itsukaichi-cho, Saeki-gun, Hiroshima Pref.	Wararu, Peru, South America	Land owner	EQ-89-1
	*Family * wife: Misako; first son: Yoshiji; second son: Yasuji; first daughter: Takeko; second daughter: Sachiko; third daughter: Eiko; fourth daughter: Itsuko			

NAGASHIMA, Koichi (51)	Kururi-cho, Kimitsu-gun, Chiba Pref.	Los Angeles, California	Business	DV-13-A
	*Family * wife: Masae; first son: Hiroshi (Frank); first daughter: Yachiyo; brother: Yasuhei			
NAITO, Takeshi (41)	Sakaegami-cho, Fukui-gun, Fukui Pref.	Lima, Peru, South America	Haberdashery	V-53
	Family * wife: Shizuko; first son: Seiichi; first daughter: Atsuko; second daughter: Noriko			
NAKACHI, Mankichi (42)	Honbu-cho, Kokuto-gun, Okinawa Pref.	Lima, Peru, South America	Café	Q-46-1
	*Family * wife: Ushi; third daughter: Teruko; fourth daughter: Ryoko; fifth daughter: Mitsuko; sixth daughter: Chiyoko			
NAKAGAWA, Yoshiro (42)	Oi-mura, Kazushi-gun, Mie Pref.	Chiclayo, Peru, South America	Barber, Beauty salon	V-29
	*Family * first son: Kazuo			
NAKAHARA, Jinnosuke (67)	Nishiwakino-mura, Umikusa-gun, Wakayama Pref.	San Francisco, California	Hotel	T-4-B
	*Family * wife: Tamae			
NAKAHARA, Chikamasa (41)	Kokuto-mura, Kokuto-gun, Okinawa Pref.	Kaiyao, Peru, South America	Haberdashery	V-61
	*Family * wife: Haru; first son: Chikanori; second son: Masaharu; third son: Mitsuo			

(*continued*)

CRYSTAL CITY REGISTRY JAPANESE FAMILY LIST February 11 1945 *(continued)*

Name (Age)	Primary Address	Previous Address	Occupation	Section No.
NAKAHARA, Toshiharu (43)	Nishiwakino-mura, Umikusa-gun, Wakayama Pref.	San Francisco, California	Hotel	D-14-B
	*Family * wife: Kimie; first daughter: Yaeko; second daughter: Nobuko; third daughter: Tomoko			
NAKAKU, Yoshinao (43)	Nago-cho, Kokuto-gun, Okinawa Pref.	Kaiyao, Peru, South America	Material shop	DV-107
	*Family * wife: Oshi; first son: Mitsuo; second son: Shigeru; third son: Jun; fourth son: Tadashi; fifth son: Mitsugu; sixth son: Tsutomu; second daughter: Sumiko; third daughter: Kaneko			
NAKAMATSU, Yayasu (47)	Nakajo-mura, Chuto-gun, Okinawa Pref.	Lima, Peru, South America	Material shop	DV-104
	*Family * wife: Kameo; second son: Morimitsu; third son: Norimori; fourth son: Moriharu; fifth son: Masakichi; fourth daughter: Sueko; fifth daughter: Shizue			
NAKMATSU, Yamitsu (35)	Nakajo-mura, Chuto-gun, Okinawa Pref.	Kaiyao, Peru, South America	Material shop	V-73
	*Family * wife: Natsue			
NAKAMOTO, Tomoyoshi (40)	Nishishin-machi, Naha-city, Okinawa Pref.	Lima, Peru, South America	Business	D-2-B
	*Family * wife: Hatsuko; first son: Koichi; first daughter: Teruko; second daughter: Reiko			

NAKAMURA, Kengoro (54)	Hanechi-mura, Kokuto-gun, Okinawa Pref.	Los Angeles, California	Legal office clerk	EQ-80-3
	*Family * first son: Akira; second son: Masao; first daughter: Mitsuko			
NAKAMURA, Hachiyoshi (50)	Mansei-cho, Kawabe-gun, Kagoshima Pref.	Kaiyao, Peru, South America	Haberdashery	Q-57-3
	*Family * wife: Harue; first son: Yoshihisa; second son: Sumihisa; first daughter: Toshiko; second daughter: Taeko			
NAKAMURA, Yoshijuro (47)	Ina-mura, Aichi-gun, Shiga Pref.	Balanco, Peru, South America	Business	V-17,18
	*Family * wife: Sumako; first son: Yoshiaki; second son: Yoshikazu; third son: Hiroshi; first daughter: Kazuko; second daughter: Masako; third daughter: Aiko			
NAKAMURA, Katsuei (57)	Tauakura-cho, Higashishirakawa-gun, Fukushima Pref.	Torjillo, Peru, South America	Agriculture	V-45,46
	*Family * wife: Victoria; first son: Leonardo; second son: Julio; third son: Telesita; first daughter: Grashef; second daughter: Lolita;			
NAKATOMOE, Shiro (52)	Mukaihara-mura, Takada-gun, Hiroshima Pref.	Seattle, Washington	Business	T-55-A
	*Family * wife: Chieko; first son: Souichiro; second daughter: Sumiko			

(*continued*)

CRYSTAL CITY REGISTRY JAPANESE FAMILY LIST February 11 1945 *(continued)*

Name (Age)	Primary Address	Previous Address	Occupation	Section No.
NAKAMURA, Tatsushi (39)	Tafuse-mura, Hioki-gun, Kagoshima Pref.	Los Angeles, California	Hotel	Q-66-1
	*Family * wife: Kikuko; first daughter: Ruriko; second daughter: Keiko			
NAKANISHI, Eitaro (58)	Tanami-mura, Nishimui-gun, Wakayama Pref.	Guadalupe, California	Agriculture	T-49-B
	*Family * wife: Shizuko			
NAKANO, Kenichi (41)	Kuzushiro-mura, Chikujo-gun, Fukuoka Pref.	Chico, California	Business	Q-54-3
	*Family * wife: Mizuko; first daughter: Emiko; third daughter: Kazumi			
NAKANO, Kiichi (35)	Ouchi-mura, Yoshiki-gun, Yamaguchi Pref.	Arekiga, Peru, South America	Business	Q-42-4
	*Family * wife: Kikuyo			
NAKAO, Iwazo (32)	Jinho-cho, Hiroshima-city, Hiroshima Pref.	Lima, Peru, South America	Business	Q-48-4
	*Family * wife: Yoshie; first daughter: Keiko; second daughter: Reiko			
NAKAJIMA, Koyoji (57)	Takamichi-mura, Tamana-gun, Kumamoto Pref.	Lima, Peru, South America	Fabric shop	D-23-B
	*Family * wife: Sawa; second son: Shintaro; third son: Hiroshi			

NAKAJMA, Sadajiro (51)	Niiyama-mura, Kanzaki-gun, Saga Pref.	Seattle, Washington	Business	V-121
	*Family * wife: Shieko; second son: Daisuke; first daughter: Kazuko			
NAKAJIMA, Shizuo (47)	Kinosho-machi, Fukuyama-city, Hiroshima Pref.	Guadalupe, California	Fertilizer business	D-37-B
	*Family * wife: Teruko; first son: Katsuaki; second son: Yuji; first daughter: Kimie			
NAKASONE, Katsujiro (42)	Honbu-cho, Kokuto-gun, Okinawa Pref.	Lima, Peru, South America	Business	Q-62-1
	*Family * wife, Makato; first daughter: Mitsuko			
NAKATA, Shigeyoshi (42)	Rokui-mura, Asa-gun, Hiroshima Pref.	Monte Bello, California	Agriculture	D-25-A
	*Family * wife: Sumiko; first son: Kazuma; second son: Shigeo; third son: Itsuo; first daughter: Shigeko; second daughter: Michiko			
NAKAYAMA, Chiyomatsu (58)	Yoshifuji-mura, Kitauwa-gun, Ehime Pref.	Hauha, Peru, South America	Business	EQ-88-1
	*Family * wife: Kinue; first son: Yoshihisa; second son: Katsuma; first daughter: Yasuko; second daughter: Mutsuko			
NISHI, Fumihachi (45)	Taichi-cho, Higashimui-gun, Wakayama Pref	San Diego, California	Fishery	D-45-1
	*Family * none			

(*continued*)

CRYSTAL CITY REGISTRY JAPANESE FAMILY LIST February 11 1945 *(continued)*

Name (Age)	Primary Address	Previous Address	Occupation	Section No.
NISHII, Hirochika (42)	Takase-cho, Tamana-gun, Kumamoto Pref.	San Diego, California	Missionary	D-30-B
	*Family * wife: Nobue; third son: Watahiro; second daughter: Akiko			
NISHIJIMA, Shuzo (55)	Moto-mura, Tamana-gun, Kumamoto Pref.	Sacramento, California	Business	Q-71-4
	*Family * wife: Kumano; first son: Hiroya			
NISHIKAWA, Kiichiro (57)	Saiku-cho, Akashi-city, Hyogo Pref.	West Morland, California	Agriculture	D-21-A
	*Family * wife: Ai; second son: Takashi; third son: Isao			
NISHIMUTA, Sumitaka (43)	Eimei-mura, Yushuku-gun, Kagoshima Pref.	Wacho, Peru, South America	Carpenter	EQ-73-4
	*Family * wife: Eda			
NISHINA, Seizo (41)	Mita-mura, Takada-gun, Hiroshima Pref.	Los Angeles, California	Gardener	D-12-A
	*Family * wife: Kiyoka; first son: Katsuhiro; first daughter: Ruriko			
NISHINAGA, Shiro (49)	Kanda-mura, Toyoura-gun, Yamaguchi Pref.	Suyana, Peru, South America	Business	V-58
	*Family * wife: Miyoko; first son: Junpei; second son: Tatsusuke; third son: Akio			

NISHINO, Kosaku (55)	Toshida-mura, Nakashingawa-gun, Toyama Pref.	Portland, Oregon	Business	DV-97-A
	*Family * wife: Ayako			
NISHINO, Yoshio (35)	Mitani-mura, Oda-gun, Okayama Pref.	Balanco, Peru, South America	Haberdashery	D-31-B
	*Family * wife: Chieko; second daughter: Kimiko; third daughter: Yoko			
NISHIOKA, Kazuto (44)	Yoshida-mura, Takada-gun, Hiroshima Pref.	Clarksburg, California	Contractor	T-16-BC
	*Family * wife: Kofumi; first son: Mikio; second son: Tadao; first daughter: Fumie			
NISHITANI, Hideto (43)	Saka-mura, Aki-gun, Hiroshima Pref.	Lima, Peru, South America	Poultry farming	Q-71-1
	*Family * wife: Makiko; first son: Terutaka; second son: Sumi; third son: Hiroshi; fourth son: Kenji; fifth son: Eigo; sixth son: Hidezo; first daughter: Yasuko			
NOGAWA, Hiroshi (40)	Nakakamoda, Kamoda-ku, Tokyo	Los Angeles, California	Trade company member	DV-140-B
	*Family * wife: Kikue; first son: Masaaki			
NOGUNI, Kame (51)	Ginowan-mura, Chuto-gun, Okinawa Pref.	Supe, Peru, South America	Haberdashery	DV-106
	*Family * wife: Kame; first son: Hiroshi; second son: Sadao; first daughter: Nobuko; second daughter: Yoshiko			

(*continued*)

CRYSTAL CITY REGISTRY JAPANESE FAMILY LIST February 11 1945 *(continued)*

Name (Age)	Primary Address	Previous Address	Occupation	Section No.
NOIKE, Takeji (44)	Omori-mura, Nobuo-gun, Fukushima Pref.	Lima, Peru, South America	Hardware seller	T-5-A
	*Family * wife: Chiyoko; first son: Tadao; first daughter: Hisako; second daughter: Setsuko; third daughter: Mitsuko			
NOMACHI, Tamanosuke (59)	Anauchi-mura, Aki-gun, Kochi Pref.	Glendale, Arizona	Missionary	EQ-80-2
	*Family * wife: Akie; first daughter: Minoe			
NONOGUCHI, Chiyoichi (50)	Kamo-mura, Tsubo-gun, Okayama Pref.	Los Angeles, California	Gardener	D-33-A
	*Family * wife: Matsuyo; first son: Hajime			
NOXAKI, Kiyoshi (56)	Takaida-mura, Nakakawachi-gun, Osaka-fu	Arroyo Grande, California	Teacher	Q-44-4
	*Family * wife: Yutaka; first daughter: Yukashi; second daughter; Sumire			
(O)				
OCHIAI, Keikichi (55)	Kanaya-cho, Fujiwara-gun, Shizuoka Pref.	Hilo, Hawaii	Clerk	Q-54-1
	*Family *wife: Katsuko; first son: Takashi; second son: Toru; first daughter: Sumie; second daughter: Shizuko			

ODA, Junichi (44)	Ukui-mura, Higashimui-gun, Wakayama Pref.	Monterey, California	Canned food seller	Q-56-3
	*Family * wife: Maki; first son: Tsuneo			
ODA, Kaname (34)	Yasuno-mura, Yamagata-gun, Hiroshima Pref.	Wararu, Peru, South America	Company member	EQ-77-4
	*Family * wife: Tokiko; first daughter: Masako; second daughter: Fumiko			
ODA, Setsuji (52)	Kidtsune-mura, Kamo-gun, Horoshima Pref	Hollywood, California	Agriculture	D-53-B
	*Family * wife: Tsuneko; first son: Takayuki; second son: Nobuyoshi; first daughter: Emiko			
ODA, Zenkichi (45)	Ukui-mura, Higashimui-gun, Wakayama Pref	Lima, Peru, South America	Agriculture	DV-101
	*Family * wife: Setsue; first son: Ikuhiro; second son: Takayasu; third son: Masatoshi; first daughter: Ikuyo; second daughter: Asayo			
OGAWA, Takara (47)	Yokokawa-cho, Hiroshima-city, Hiroshima Pref	Compton, California	Agriculture	D-40-B
	*Family * wife: Iyano; first daughter: Kazuko; second daughter: Taeko; third daughter: Sumiko			
OHARA, Hideo (34)	Mitani-cho, Meguro-ku, Tokyo	Lima, Peru, South America	Teacher	EQ-73-3
	*Family * wife: Sachiko; first son: Yasuhiko; first daughter: Tamiko; second daughter: Miwako			

(*continued*)

CRYSTAL CITY REGISTRY JAPANESE FAMILY LIST February 11 1945 *(continued)*

Name (Age)	Primary Address	Previous Address	Occupation	Section No.
OHASHI, Taro (42)	Miyazu-cho, Kosha-gun, Kyoto Pref.	Lima, Peru, South America	Industry	Q-61-4
	*Family * wife: Fusae; first son: Ken; second son: Mamoru; first daughter: Miyoko			
OHASHI, Kanehiko (35)	Shokunin-cho, Maizuru-city, Kyoto-fu	Lima, Peru, South America	Business	Q-67-2
	*Family * wife: Asa; first daughter: Ayano			
OMAE, Yoshio (44)	Miwazaki, Shingu-city, Wakayama Pref.	Los Angeles, California	Manufacturer	V-117
	*Family * wife: Tamie; first son: Yoshio; first daughter: Fumiko; second daughter: Aiko; sister: OMAE, Tomiko			
OTA, Kunio(56)	Yasu-cho, Isezaki-city, Gunma Pref.	Hawaii Island, Hawaii	Missionary	T-62-A
	*Family * wife: Matsu; second daughter: Sumie; third daughter: Mieko			
OKABE, Umesaburo (57)	Heiwa-mura, Nakajima-gun, Aichi Pref.	Yolo, California	Agriculture	Q-50-1
	*Family * wife: Asao; first son: Jyoji; second son: Yoshiaki; third son: Masayuki;, fourth son: Takashi			

OKACHI, Tomohiro (56)	Etsuchi-cho, Takaoka-city, Kochi Pref.	Hilo, Hawaii	Contractor	D-45-B
	*Family * wife: Komatsu; first son: Masayuki; sixth son: Tetsuro; second daughter: Michiko; third daughter: Shigeko			
OKAMOTO, Hisajiro (58)	Fukuda-mura, Kojima-gun, Okayama Pref.	Portland, Oregon	Hotel	Q-54-4
	*Family * wife: Mitsu; first son: Taichi; first daughter: Chie			
OKAMOTO, Makitaro	Sho-mura, Kubo-gun, Okayama Pref.	Portland, Oregon	Hotel	Q-55-2
	*Family * wife: Kotoe; second son: Kenji; third son: Tadashi			
OKAMOTO, Masaru (38)	Mubeyama-mura, Ashina-gun, Hiroshima Pref.	Guadalupe, California	Agriculture	T-40-C
	*Family * wife: Shizuko			
OKAMURA, Naoei (53)	Eimei-mura, Yushuku-gun, Kagoshima Pref.	El Centro, California	Business	T-44-B
	*Family * wife: Hiroko; first son: Naohiko; second son: Toshio			
OKANO, Toumatsu (59)	Kihara-cho, Mahara-city, Hiroshima Pref.	Riverside, California	Poultry farming	EQ-95-1
	*Family * wife: Mineyo; first son: Chitose; first daughter: Yoko			

(*continued*)

CRYSTAL CITY REGISTRY JAPANESE FAMILY LIST February 11 1945 *(continued)*

Name (Age)	Primary Address	Previous Address	Occupation	Section No.
OKAZAKI, Ichimaru (50)	Mayagami-mura, Mitsu-gun, Okayama Pref.	Santa Maria, California	Owner	D-60-A
	*Family * wife: Hamako; first son: Seiji; second son: Terumi; first daughter: Maruko			
OKAZAKI, Masashi (46)	Kyoto-mura, Nakatado-gun, Kagawa Pref.	Los Angeles, California	Priest of Tenri-kyo	D-12-B
	*Family * wife: Hideko; first son: Shiro; first daughter: Kumiko; second daughter: Takako; fourth daughter: Machiko			
OKAZAKI, Kuruo (58)	Kyoto-mura, Nakatado-gun, Kagawa Pref.	Portland, Oregon	Priest of Tenri-kyo	EQ-82-3
	*Family * wife: Kunie; fourth son: Shigeru; fifth son: Kou; sixth son: Michiharu; second daughter: Tsuyako; third daughter: Yoshiko			
OKAZAKI, Yatohachi (52)	Mikawa-mura, Asa-gun, Hiroshima Pref.	San Juan Bautista, California	Agriculture	D-55-B
	*Family * wife: Miyako; second son: Akira; third son: Hideo; third daughter: Toshie; brother-in-law: OKIDO, Fukusaburo			
OKI, Kakumaro (45)	Toyama-mura, Asa-gun, Hiroshima Pref	Ervine, California	Agriculture	DV-146-A
	*Family * wife: Miyako; first daughter: Mary; second daughter: Tomoko; third daughter: Mitsuko; fourth daughter: Kimiko			

OKINAGA, Yoshio (42)	Atago-cho, Iwakuni-city, Yamaguchi Pref.	Wacho, Peru, South America	Blacksmith	D-47-B
	*Family * wife: Hatsuko; first son: Masao; second son: Tadashi; third son: Kiyoshi; first daughter: Yoshiko			
OKITA, Miyoshi (37)	Mifune-cho, Kamimasuki-gun, Kumamoto Pref.	Los Angeles, California	Missionary	Q-56-4
	*Family * wife: Chiyoko; first son: Narumi; second son: Masazumi			
OKU, Kaneyoshi (37)	Ichiki-mura, Hioki-gun, Hiroshima Pref.	La Paz, Bolivia, South America	Business	DV-135-B
	*Family * wife: Somi; first son: Yoshihiko; second son: Akio			
OKU, Toshiaki (39)	Tsunoda-mura, Chikujo-gun, Fukuoka Pref.	Southgate, California	Cleaning	DV-138-B
	*Family * wife: Hideko; first son: Toshikazu; first daughter: Yoshie			
OKURA, Kiyomichi (46)	Nishitsunoda-mura, Chikujo-gun, Fukuoka Pref.	Hawaii Island, Hawaii	Missionary	T-35-B
	*Family * wife: Kokiku; first son: Kiyoshiro; first daughter: Taeko			
OKUSHIBA, Isamu (40)	Nanbu-cho, Hidaka-gun, Wakayama Pref.	Riverside, California	Agriculture	T-51-A
	*Family * wife: Hisako; first son: Teruo; first daughter: Kiyoko; second daughter: Sumiko			

(*continued*)

CRYSTAL CITY REGISTRY JAPANESE FAMILY LIST February 11 1945 *(continued)*

Name (Age)	Primary Address	Previous Address	Occupation	Section No.
OKINAGA, Yoshihiko (48)	Hanechi-mura, Kokuto-gun, Okinawa Pref.	Lima, Peru, South America	Business	EQ-74-1
	*Family * wife: Yuki, adopted son: Yoshinori			
OSAKO, Aikichi (55)	Kasago-cho, Kawabe-gun, Kagoshima Pref.	Los Angeles, California	Business	DV-147-A
	*Family * wife: Noru; first son: Takanobu; second son: Yukio; first daughter: Tatsuko; second daughter: Etsuko; third daughter: Masako			
OSHIMA, Masao (44)	Hera-mura, Saeki-gun, Hiroshima Pref.	Arlington, California	Agriculture	D-15-A
	*Family * wife: Chiyono; first son: Hiroyuki; second son: Yoshitake; third son: Hideo; second daughter: Fujie			
OSHITA, Takeshi (45)	Ochiai-mura, Asa-gun, Hiroshima Pref.	Hoitia (Probably Whittier) California	Agriculture	T-3-ABC
	*Family * wife: Morino; first son: Hideaki; second son: Takeji; third son: Katsuaki; first daughter: Masako; second daughter: Kimiyo; third daughter: Tomoko; fourth daughter: Yasuko			
OSHIRO, Nagayuki (45)	Imakiji-mura, Kokuto-gun, Okinawa Pref.	Lima, Peru, South America	Agriculture	V-64
	*Family * wife: Shizuko; first daughter: Rumiko			

OSHITA, Saichi (54)	Shimonakagawa-cho, Kure-city, Hiroshima Pref.	Wacho, Peru, South America	Hardware seller	EQ-92-1
	*Family * wife: Toshiko; first son: Hisashi; second son: Masaaki; third son: Toshinori; fourth son: Norihiko; fifth son: Norio; first daughter: Mariko; second daughter: Midori			
OSUGA, Shinoki (62)	Nadayama-cho, Hikone-city, Shiga Pref.	Santa Maria, California	Farming business broker	T-37-C
	*Family * wife: Hatsue			
OTANI, Norimatsu (45)	Takatori-mura, Ika-gun, Shiga Pref.	Lima, Peru, South America	Import business	EQ-86-4
	*Family * wife: Harue			
OUCHI, Matsuzo (53)	Noda-mura, Nobuo-gun, Fukushima Pref.	Wacho, Peru, South America	Agriculture	DV-100
	*Family * wife: Takino; first son: Masatake; second son: Masao; third son: Hiroshi; fourth son: Yu; fifth son: Akira; sixth son: Masao; first daughter: Kaneko			
OYAKAWA, Yoshiharu (37)	Hanechi-mura, Kokuto-gun, Okinawa Pref.	Lima, Peru, South America	Haberdashery	EQ-79-2
	*Family * wife: Oto; first son: Kenichi; second son: Keiji; second daughter: Mitsuko; third daughter: Tami			

(*continued*)

CRYSTAL CITY REGISTRY JAPANESE FAMILY LIST February 11 1945 *(continued)*

Name (Age)	Primary Address	Previous Address	Occupation	Section No.
OYAKAWA, Yoshitatsu (36)	Hanechi-mura, Kokuto-gun, Okinawa Pref.	Lima, Peru, South America	Haberdashery	EQ-79-1
	*Family * wife: Yaeko; father: OYAKAWA, Yoshigoro			
OYAMA, Naganori (44)	Keitoku-mura, Yama-gun, Fukushima Pref.	Sacramento, California	Banker	D-23-A
	*Family * wife: Sachiko; first son: Chikaaki; second son: Takashi; first daughter: Toshiko; second daughter: Junko			
OYAMA, Fusakichi (39)	Higashiyama-mura, Yamakado-gun, Fukuoka Pref.	Chiclayo, Peru, South America	Business	D-3-B
	*Family *wife: Masako; first son: Yoshio; first daughter: Shizuko; second daughter: Kazuko			
OYAMA, Kuraji (45)	Higashiyama-mura, Yamakado-gun, Fukuoka Pref.	Chiclayo, Peru, South America	Business	T-53-A
	*Family * wife: Shigeno; first son: Hirome; second son: Mitsuaki; third son: Toru; fourth son: Takashi			
OZAKI, Motoichi (33)	Miwazaki, Shingu-city, Wakayama Pref.	Lima, Peru, South America	Business	Q-53-3
	*Family * wife: Tamiyo; first son: Kuniaki; first daughter: Masako			

OZAKI, Jinpachi (52)	Nodaya-cho, Okayama-city, Okayama Pref.	Mackiegille (sic), Nevada	Business	T-38-B
	*Family * wife: Sono			
OZAKI, Shintaro (58)	Miwazaki, Shingu-city, Wakayama Pref.	Terminal Island, California	Fishery	Q-53-3
	*Family * none			
(S)				
SAHASHI, Tadaji (32)	Komaki-mura, Higashikasugai-gun, Aichi Pref.	La Paz, Bolivia, South America	Business	T-2-B
	*Family * wife: Masae; first daughter: Michiko			
SAEKI, Masao (51)	Yashiro-mura, Kumage-gun, Yamaguchi Pref.	Tana, Peru, South America	Material shop	V-80
	*Family * wife: Mitsuko			
SAITO, Seigan (52)	Katagami-mura, Imadate-gun, Fukui Pref.	Honolulu, Hawaii	Missionary	D-47-A
	*Family * wife: Naruo; first son: Yoshikazu; first daughter: Nobuko; second daughter: Keiko			
SAKAI, Kunisuke (45)	Mioka-mura, Kumage-gun, Yamaguchi Pref.	Maui, Hawaii	Priest	T-47-B
	*Family * wife: Fujie; first daughter: Yuriko			

(*continued*)

CRYSTAL CITY REGISTRY JAPANESE FAMILY LIST February 11 1945 *(continued)*

Name (Age)	Primary Address	Previous Address	Occupation	Section No.
SAKAIRI, Takeo (46)	Ueno-mura, Makabe-gun, Ibaragi Pref.	Lima, Peru, South America	Agriculture	EQ-89-3
	*Family * wife: Yasuko; first son: Takeyasu; second son: Sadao; third son: Yasuo; first daughter: Michiko; second daughter: Takeko; third daughter: Eiko; fourth daughter: Hitoko			
SAKAMAKI, Sueharu (62)	Watachi-cho, Tsu-city, Mie Pref.	San Francisco, California	Trade business	T-17-BC
	*Family * wife: Teru; first son: Yukiharu; second son: Motoharu; third son: Masaharu; first daughter: Marie			
SAKAMOTO, Harue (45)	Kuga-cho, Kuga-gun, Yamaguchi Pref.	Lima, Peru, South America	N/A	Q-50-3
	*Family * third son: Mitsuaki; fourth son: Hideaki			
SAKAMOTO, Susumu (45)	Takaishi-mura, Takaoka-gun, Kochi Pref.	Nailis (sic), California	Agriculture	T-52-A
	*Famiy * wife: Hisaka; first son: Keiji; first daughter: Michiyo			
SASAKI, Kamekichi (65)	Hino-mura, Hino-gun, Tottori Pref.	Calexico, California	Agriculture	EQ-81-2
	*Family * wife: Yae; first daughter: Sachiko			

SASAKI, Tatsunaga (40)	Isotsu-mura, Nishiuwa-gun, Ehime Pref.	Lima, Peru, South America	Watchmaker	Q-59-3
	*Family * wife: Fumie; first son: Genzo; second son: Tatsuo; third son: Masanori; fourth son: Masakatsu; third daughter: Michiko; fourth daughter: Hideko; fifth daughter: Ayako			
SATO, Hiroji (43)	Seta-mura, Kikuchi-gun, Kumamoto Pref.	Chiclayo, Peru, South America	Pottery seller	Q-59-1
	*Family * wife: Sue; first son: Shigeru			
SATO, Kanezo (35)	Mutsuai-mura, Date-gun, Fukushima Pref.	Lima, Peru, South America	Business	Q-61-3
	*Family * wife: Kin; first son: Yoshiaki; first daughter: Kimiko			
SATO, Kumakichi (41)	Misawa-mura, Nachishi-gun, Yamagata Pref.	Wankaiyo, Peru, South America	Hotel	EQ-86-1
	*Family * wife: Natsu; first son: Iwao; second son: Sojiro; third son: Masukuni; first daughter: Naoko; second daughter: Yoshiko; third daughter: Miyoko.			
SATO, Masao (27)	Kuwaori-cho, Date-gun, Fukushima Pref.	Lima, Peru, South America	Shop clerk	EQ-86-3
	*Family * wife: Tai			
SATO, Tadao (42)	Tasumaru-cho, Ukiwa-gun, Fukuoka Pref.	San Lorenzo, California	Agriculture	D-7-B
	*Family * wife: Fumiko; first son: Tsuneo; second son: Shigeru; first daughter: Reiko			

(continued)

CRYSTAL CITY REGISTRY JAPANESE FAMILY LIST February 11 1945 *(continued)*

Name (Age)	Primary Address	Previous Address	Occupation	Section No.
SAWAMURA, Shigenori (46)	Takaoka-cho, Takaoka-gun, Kochi Pref.	Woodland, California	Agriculture	T-41-A
	*Family * wife: Inami; first son: Hideo; fourth daughter: Kyoko			
SAWATAKI, Tetsuzo (56)	Kmakoshi-cho, Shimizu-city, Shizuoka Pref.	Los Angeles, California	Business	T-33-B
	*Family * wife: Masu; first son: Masuji			
SERA, Katsutaro (44)	Ichikawa-mura, Takada-gun, Hiroshima Pref.	Sacramento, California	Agriculture	Q-42-3
	*Family * wife: Chizu			
SHIBATA, Nobu (55)	Shimizu-cho, Shimizu-city, Shizuoka Pref.	Long Beach, California	Sea products trading	T-57-A
	*Family * wife: Kumi; first son: Tomio; second son: Jun			
SHIBAYAMA, Yuzo (39)	Tateishi-mura, Asakura-gun, Fukuoka Pref.	Lima, Peru, South America	Import business	EQ-74-3
	*Family * wife: Tatsue; first son: Isamu; second son: Kenichi; third son: Ken; first daughter: Fusako; second daughter: Kikue; third daughter: Akiko.			

SHIGA, Yoshisada (38)	Machimi-mura, Nishiuwa-gun, Ehime Pref.	Hauha, Peru, South America	Business	EQ-73-1
	*Family * wife: Masako; other: SUEMATSU, Shizuko; SUEMATSU, Teruko; SUEMATSU, Shokichi			
SHIMA, Miyotaro (51)	Kushige-mura, Yame-gun, Fukuoka Pref.	Torjillo, Peru, South America	Business	Q-64-1
	*Family * wife: Hisae; first son: Tamotsu; first daughter: Kuniko			
SHIMABUKURO, Takichi (39)	Hanechi-mura, Kokuto-gun, Okinawa Pref.	Lima, Peru, South America	Milk shop	DV-102
	*Family * wife: Matsu; first son: Ikuo; second son: Mitsuaki; third son: Minoru; first daughter: Tatsuko; second daughter: Shizuko			
SHIMABUKURO, Taro (46)	Hanechi-mura, Kokuto-gun, Okinawa Pref	Lima, Peru, South America	Material shop	V-122
	*Family * second son: Yukinori; second daughter: Teruko			
SHIMABARA, Sekijiro (51)	Itsukaichi-cho, Saeki-gun, Hiroshima Pref.	Los Angeles, California	Hotel	EQ-93-1
	*Family * first son: Tatsuo; second son: Akimitsu; first daughter: Kazuko; mother-in-law: MITSUMUNE, Haya; brother-in-law: MITSUMUNE, Akira			

(*continued*)

CRYSTAL CITY REGISTRY JAPANESE FAMILY LIST February 11 1945 *(continued)*

Name (Age)	Primary Address	Previous Address	Occupation	Section No.
SHIMAKAWA, Hideo (44)	Yagiso-mura, Aichi-gun, Shiga Pref.	Santa Barbara, California	Missionary	Q-45-4
	*Family * wife: Tomiko; first son: Hidetada; first daughter: Yoko			
SHIMIZU, Sengo (38)	Moto-mura, Hiba-gun, Hiroshima Pref.	Salinas, California	Agriculture	D-51-B
	*Family * wife: Haruko; first son: Akito; second son: Teruaki; third son: Koichi; first daughter: Reiko			
SHIMIZU, Susumu (38)	Nagataba-mura, Asa-gun, Hiroshima Pref.	Lima, Peru, South America	Fuel seller	Q-67-3
	*Family * wife: Tamao			
SHINO, Tamori (59)	Inaokaminami-mura, Kume-gun, Okayama Pref.	Los Angeles, California	Business	EQ-81-1
	*Family * wife: Yoshiko			
SHIMOIDA, Kazuo (33)	Iida-city, Nagano Pref.	Kochabamba, Bolivia, South America	Shop Clerk	DV-139-A
	*Family * wife: Tomiko			

[illegible]	Mizoguchi-cho, Hino-gun, Tottori Pref.	Oakland, California	Gardener	D-5-B
	*Family * wife: Kayo; first son: Shunji; first daughter: Takako; second daughter: Sumiko; third daughter: Makiko			
SHIOZAKI, Takayoshi (45)	Ukui-mura, Higashimui-gun, Wakayama Pref.	Lompoc, California	N/A	D-10-B
	*Family * wife: Chiyo; first son: Isamu; second son: Yutaka			
SHIROTA, Torajiro (74)	Kamigo-mura, Shimoina-gun, Nagano Pref.	Los Angeles, California	Priest of Tenri-kyo	T-54-C
	*Family * wife: Iseyo			
SOYAMA, Kenzo (55)	Kokubo-cho, Shira-gun, Kagoshima Pref.	Visalia, California	Business	EQ-95-4
	*Family * wife: Fuku; first son: Akinori			
SUGANO, Tadaichi (39)	Kihata-mura, Adachi-gun, Fukushima Pref.	Sermal, California	Agriculture	D-48-B
	*Family * wife: Sadako; first son: Tadao; second son: Kenji; third son: Shoichi; fourth son: Kazuo; first daughter: Kei			
SUGANO, Yahichi (46)	Shiozawa-mura, Adachi-gun, Fukushima Pref.	Wacho, Peru, South America	Business	Q-67-1
	*Family * wife: You; first daughter: Kuniko			

(continued)

CRYSTAL CITY REGISTRY JAPANESE FAMILY LIST February 11 1945 (*continued*)

Name (Age)	Primary Address	Previous Address	Occupation	Section No.
SUGIYAMA, Shigeru (54)	Nishikawa-mura, Kume-gun, Okayama Pref.	Lima, Peru, South America	Pottery seller	V-33,34
	*Family * Hideko; first son: Takehi; second son: Yasushi; third son: Akira; first daughter: Shigeko			
SUMI, Shiyomichi (45)	Sakitsu-mura, Shieki-gun, Tottori Pref.	Redondo Beach, California	Agriculture	T-43-A
	*Family * wife: Haruko; first son: Norimichi; first daughter: Akiko; second daughter: Nobuko			
SUMIYOSHI, Ichizaemon (66)	Kajiki-cho, Shira-gun, Kagoshima Pref.	San Diego, California	Agriculture	Q-52-4
	*Family * wife: Kin; fourth daughter: Meriko			
SUZUKI, Kin (43)	Sotosodeshi-mura, Shimizu-city, Shizuoka Pref.	Wankaio, Peru, South America	Agriculture	Q-52-4
	*Family * first son: Manabu; third daughter: Hiromi; fourth daughter: Suzuko; fifth daughter: Masumi; sixth daughter: Chieko; mother: Kane.			
SUZUKI, Hiroshi (50)	Setagaya-cho, Yodobashi-ku, Tokyo	Los Angeles, California	Newspaper writer	D-1-B
	*Family * wife: Teru; first daughter: Tami			

(T)				
TAGASHIRA, Yoshio (51)	Tenma-cho, Hiroshima-city, Hiroshima Pref.	Honolulu, Hawaii	Business	Q-41-4
	*Family * wife: Tomoe; first son: Yoshiyuki; first daughter: Toshiko; second daughter: Masako			
TAGUCHI, Genpei (48)	Etajima-cho, Aki-gun, Hiroshima Pref.	La Jolla, California	Agriculture	T-57-C
	*Family * wife: Koyo			
TAHARASAKO, Kinji (54)	Shishuku-cho, Yushuku-gun, Kagoshima Pref.	Visco, Peru, South America	Bar	V-21
	*Family * wife: Take			
TACHII, Hiroo (47)	Yano-cho, Aki-gun, Hiroshima Pref.	Calexico, California	Agriculture	V-113
	*Family * wife: Sadako; second son: Shigeru; third son: Hiroshi			
TAKADA, Hojun (49)	Yoshimatsu-mura, Shira-gun, Kagoshima Pref.	Gardena, California	Agriculture	DV-150-A
	*Family * wife: Tomie; second son: Takahiro; third son: Michihiro; fourth son: Yoshihiro; fifth son: Yorihiro			

(*continued*)

CRYSTAL CITY REGISTRY JAPANESE FAMILY LIST February 11 1945 (*continued*)

Name (Age)	Primary Address	Previous Address	Occupation	Section No.
TAKAHASHI, Masao (50)	Higashiyonban-cho, Sendai-city, Miyagi Pref.	Seattle, California	Contractor	T-24-BC
	*Family * wife: Hisako; first daughter: Kazuko; second daughter: Tamae; third daughter: Masako; fourth daughter: Midori			
TAKAHASHI, Sadaei (57)	Iwatsuki-mura, Yama-gun, Fukushima Pref.	Torjillo, Peru, South America	Material shop	V-15,16
	*Family * wife: Seki; first son: Kisaburo; second son: Chushiro; third son: Sueo; first daughter: Sadako; second daughter: Haruko			
TAKAHASHI, Narimichi (41)	Waizumi-mura, Micho-gun, Hiroshima Pref.	Los Angeles, California	Missionary	Q-45-2
	*Family * wife: Suzue; first son: Katsuaki; second son: Takashige; first daughter: Kyoko; second daughter: Yoshiko			
TAKAMINE, Yoshiichi (47)	Kawakami-mura, Houtaku-gun, Kumamoto Pref.	Long Beach, California	Agriculture	DV-142
	*Family * wife: Asae; first son: Kiyonori; fourth son: Takashi; fifth son: Junichi; first daughter: Chizuko; second daughter: Ayako; third daughter: Michiko; fourth daughter: Noriko; fifth daughter: Katsuko; sixth daughter: Hideko; seventh daughter: Tomiko			

TAKASHIMA, Katsue (65)	Takeshimo-mura, Adachi-gun, Fukushima Pref.	Chula Vista, California	Agriculture	T-30-B
	*Family * wife: Tsumi			
TAKAMORI, Kantaro (55)	Kawamoto-mura, Toyoda-gun, Hiroshima Pref.	La Paz, Bolivia, South America	Business	T-4-C
	*Family * Shoma			
TAKEDA, Hiroji (34)	Minamisaigo-mura, Sanpo-gun, Fukui Pref.	Woodland, California	Agriculture	T-47-A
	*Family * wife: Yoshiko; first daughter: Maruko; second daughter: Sachiko; third daughter: Michiko			
TAKEDA, Shizuma (43)	Yamamoto-mura, Shikamoto-gun, Kumamoto Pref.	Lima, Peru, South America	Barber	DV-143
	*Family * wife: Teruko; first son: Shoji; second son: Akio; first daughter: Takako; second daughter: Toshiko; third daughter: Kazuko			
TAKEI, Tokiji (41)	Asakura-cho, Asakura-gun, Fukuoka Pref.	Maui, Hawaii	Teacher	T-15-A
	*Family * wife: Yoshiko; first son: Yoshimitsu; first daughter: Junko			
TAKEMA, Shiro (43)	Hara-cho, Koishigawa-ku, Tokyo	Wacho, Peru, South America	Teacher	Q-62-3
	*Family * wife: Misao; first son: Kiyoji; first daughter: Fumie			

(*continued*)

CRYSTAL CITY REGISTRY JAPANESE FAMILY LIST February 11 1945 *(continued)*

Name (Age)	Primary Address	Previous Address	Occupation	Section No.
TAKETOMO, Mataemon (63)	Ikeda-mura, Naga-gun, Wakayama Pref.	Santa Maria, California	Agriculture	DV-94-B
	*Family * wife: Chiyoe; first son: Masao; second son: Tamio; third son: Teruo; first daughter: Haruko			
TAKEMOTO, Shinya (39)	Fukagawa-mura, Asa-gun, Hiroshima Pref.	Los Angeles, California	Hotel	T-51-B
	*Family * wife: Fumie; first daughter: Sumiko; second daughter: Mitsuyo; third daughter: Momoyo; fourth daughter: Setsuko			
TAKEI, Tsuyoshi (45)	Muro-machi, Shimomatsu-city, Yamaguchi Pref.	Oahu, Hawaii	Teacher	T-49-A
	*Family * wife: Shige; second son: Koukaku; second daughter: Michiko			
TAKEUCHI, Mokuhei (46)	Wagu-cho, Shima-gun, Mie Pref.	Los Angeles, California	Hotel	D-42-A
	*Family * wife: Mie; first son: Takashi; first daughter: Miyoko; second daughter: Keiko; third daughter: Tomoko; fourth daughter: Itsuko			
TAKEUCHI, Jingo (56)	Otsu-cho, Kikuchi-gun, Kumamoto Pref.	El Balado, California	Teacher	D-24-A
	*Family * wife: Kiwa; third son: Shozo; fourth son: Keigo; fifth son: Goro; sixth son: Akira			

TAKEUCHI, Takashi (30)	Kikusui-cho, Minato-ku, Kobe-city, Hyogo Pref.	Cochabamba, Bolivia, South America	Business	T-1-A
	*Family * wife: Nuiko; first son: Tsutomu; first daughter: Yoko			
TAMAKI, Yoshio (44)	Kitajima-cho, Wakayama-city, Wakayama Pref.	Culver City, California	Agriculture	D-52-B
	*Family * wife: Shizuko; first son: Yu; second son: Yoshifushi; first daughter: Hisako			
TAMANAHA, Sadaji (38)	Ginowan-mura, Chuto-gun, Okinawa Pref.	Lima, Peru, South America	Material shop	V-62
	*Family * wife: Yasuko; first daughter: Hiromi; second daughter: Michiko			
TAMBARA, Senkichi (53)	Hiratsu-mura, Mitsu-gun, Okayama Pref.	Portland, Oregon	Restaurant	D-53-A
	*Family * wife: Masano; first son: Toshio; second son: Ken; first daughter: Sumiko			
TAMEKUNI, Masanori (39)	Tokiwa-mura, Tau-gun, Fukui Pref.	Hawaii Island, Hawaii	Missionary	D-30-A
	*Family * wife: Matsue; first son: Masaki; second son: Kazumi; first daughter: Sachie; second daughter: Yoshie; third daughter: Hanae			
TANABE, Itsuki (54)	Kattomi-mura, Houtaku-gun, Kumamoto Pref.	Lima, Peru, South America	Bakery	EQ-75-2
	*Family * wife: Yoso			

(*continued*)

CRYSTAL CITY REGISTRY JAPANESE FAMILY LIST February 11 1945 *(continued)*

Name (Age)	Primary Address	Previous Address	Occupation	Section No.
TANABE, Sadayuki (49)	Hama-cho, Kamimasuki-gun, Kumamoto Pref.	Lima, Peru, South America	Business	T-26-B
	*Family * wife: Tomo			
TANAKA, Haru (51)	Etajima-mura, Aki-gun, Hiroshima Pref.	Oahu, Hawaii	Teacher	T-46-C
	*Family * none			
TANI, Dentaro (54)	Oshima-mura, Higashimui-gun, Wakayama Pref.	Terminal Island, California	Fishery	DV-126-B
	*Family * wife: Yuwae; first son: Tetsuo; second son: Joji; third son: Toshiro			
TANIGUCHI, Isamu (49)	Tatsukado-mura, Naga-gun, Wakayama Pref.	Brentwood, California	Agriculture	T-46-B
	*Family * Wife: Sadayo; second son: Izumi			
TANIGUCHI, Masakiyo (52)	Hachi-mura, Sampo-gun, Fukui Pref.	Piura, Peru, South America	Watchmaker	V-25,26
	*Family * wife: Masu; firt son: Mitsuo; first daughter: Fumiko, second daughter: Yukie; third daughter: Mieko; fourth daughter: Shizuka			

TANIGUCHI, Hiroaki (47)	Iimuro-mura, Asa-gun, Hiroshima Pref	Sebastopol, California	Agriculture	D-36-A
	*Family * wife: Shigeko; first son: Hiroshi; second son: Mikio; first daughter: Kumiko			
TANIGUCHI, Yoichi (44)	Iimuro-mura, Asa-gun, Hiroshima Pref.	Sebastopol, California	Dry fruit manufacture	D-36-B
	*Family * wife: Ayami; first daughter: Michiko; second daughter: Kazuko			
TANIGUCHI, Takezo (54)	Kukuno-mura, Ono-gun, Gifu Pref.	San Diego, California	Business	T-44-C
	*Family * wife: Sumie			
TANIMOTO, Tsunezo (48)	Yano-cho, Aki-gun, Hiroshima Pref.	Gardena, California	Agriculture	T-28-A
	*Family * wife: Mine; first son: Tatsuo; first daughter: Tokiko			
TANINO, Yoshitaro (34)	Isozu-mura, Nishiuwa-gun, Aichi Pref.	Lima, Peru, South America	Industry	T-12-BC
	*Family * wife: Yuriko; first son: Kokichi; second son: Noboru; third son: Hiroaki; fourth son: Haruaki			
TANIOKA, Shigejiro (44)	Kusakabe-cho, Shodo-gun, Kagawa Pref.	San Francisco, California	Househusband	Q-47-3
	*Family * wife: Yuki			

(continued)

CRYSTAL CITY REGISTRY JAPANESE FAMILY LIST February 11 1945 (*continued*)

Name (Age)	Primary Address	Previous Address	Occupation	Section No.
TAOKA, Tatsuo (40)	Jinho-cho, Hiroshima-city, Hiroshima Pref.	Lima, Peru, South America	Business	D-31-A
	*Family * wife: Suzue; first son: Hozumi; first daughter: Otoe; second daughter: Shiemi; third daughter: Midori; fourth daughter: Tomiko			
TAWARA, Kotaro (49)	Wakajima-mura, Yashiro-gun, Kumamoto Pref.	Kaniete, Peru, south America	Material shop	V-23
	*Family * wife: Kiwa; first son: Toshiharu; second son: Tsuhimitsu; third son: Akio; first daughter: Sumiko; second daughter: Kiyoko			
TENTANI, Yoshisaku (47)	Masuge-cho, Amashiokunimauge-gun, Hokkaido	Lima, Peru, South America	Phermacy owner	EQ-87-1
	*Family * wife: Misao; first son: Usaku; second son: Daisaku; third son: Shosaku; first daughter: Fumiko			
TEJIMA, Shou (35)	Daifuku-mura, Asakura-gun, Fukuoka Pref.	Lima, Peru, South America	Poultry farming	V-28
	*Family * sister: ETO, Some; nephew: ETO, Yoshimitsu; MATSUDA, Tomoji; niece: ETO, Nobuko			
TOCHIO, Yasujiro (54)	Ogami-cho, Yokohama-city, Kanagawa Pref.	Arecipa, Peru, South America	Business	T-10-BC
	*Family * wife: Louisa; first son: Umbert; first daughter: Merry; second daughter: Teresa			

TODA, Yasuo (42)	Ichinomiya-mura, Hinhan-gun, Aichi Pref.	Honolulu, Hawaii	Missionary	D-49-B
	*Family * wife: Yoshie; first son: Yasuaki; first daughter: Akiko; second daughter: Shinobu			
TODOROKI, Shisei (43)	Higashi-machi, Chiyuki, Fukuoka-city, Fukuoka Pref.	San Luis, Califonia	Missionary	DV-97
	*Family * wife: Tomo; second son: Hiromitsu; first daughter: Reiko; second daughter: Yoko			
TOMIHAMA, Munemutsu (44)	Nakajo-mura, Chuto-gun, Okinawa Pref.	Wacho, Peru, South America	Agriculture	V-77
	*Family * wife: Kame; first daughter; Hatsuko			
TORIU, Tsurukichi (44)	Hayamahama-cho, Echiwa-gun, Ehime Pref.	Chiclayo, Peru, South America	Teacher	Q-59-3
	*Family * wife: Kikuko; first son: Akihiro; first daughter: Yasuko			
TORIE, Toshihide (40)	Shikajima-cho, Kohana-ku, Osaka fu	Hillsborough, California	N/A	S-115
	*Family * wife: Yoshiko			
TORISAWA, Rinzo (58)	Joto-mura, Kamo-gun, Shizuoka Pref.	Los Angeles, Caifornia	Priest of Tenri-kyo	D-16-A
	*Family * wife: Kiyo, second daughter: Setsuko, granddaughter: Chiyoko			

(*continued*)

CRYSTAL CITY REGISTRY JAPANESE FAMILY LIST February 11 1945 *(continued)*

Name (Age)	Primary Address	Previous Address	Occupation	Section No.
TORISAWA, Shigenari (35)	Joto-mura, Kamo-gun, Shizuoka Pref.	Los Angeles, California	Priest of Tenri-kyo	T-31-B
	*Family * wife: Itsuko			
TOYAMA, Masahide (43)	Ogimi-mura, Kokuto-gun, Okinawa Pref.	Kaiyao, Peru, South America	Barber	V-43,44
	*Family * wife: Ume; first son: Tetsuo; second son: Takeshi; third son: Hiromasa; first daughter: Hideko; second daughter: Emiko; third daughter: Masako; fourth daughter: Eiko			
TSUBOTA, Ryosaku (57)	Hiroshima-city, Hiroshima Pref.	Arlington, California	Agriculture	Q-49-4
	*Family * wife: Masa; second son: Masami; third son: Noboru; fourth son: Tatsumi			
TSUCHIYA, Yasuo (45)	Takashima-cho, Higashichishi-gun, Yamagata Pref.	Lima, Peru, Suth America	Business	DV-99
	*Family * wife: Harue; first son: Chikara; second son: Shigeru; third son: Tatsuo; first daughter: Miyoko; second daughter: Yoshiko; third daughter: Kazuko; fourth daughter: Hisae; fifth daughter: Yasuko			
TAKUUE, Yoshihiro (36)	Ihara-mura, Tomochi-gun, Shimane Pref.	Hawaii Island, Hawaii	Missionary	T-54-B
	*Family * wife: Hatsuko; first son: Teruyoshi			

TSUIDA, Motosuke (48)	Inahara-mura, Hidaka-gun, Wakayama Pref.	San Diego, California	Fishery	EQ-95-3
	*Family * wife: Namie; third daughter: Hideko			
TSUMAGARI, Takeji (55)	Kokubu-cho, Shira-gun, Kagoshima Pref.	San Diego, California	Hotel	T-36-C
	*Family * wife: Fuyu			
TSUNODA, Kamekichi (54)	Ota-mura, Azuma-gun, Gunma Pref.	San Diego, California	Grocery	T-54-A
	*Family * wife: Kane; first son: Susumu; first daughter: Fumiko			
TSUNODA, Kensaku (43)	Shikishima-mura, Seta-gun, Gunma Pref.	Honolulu, Hawaii	Hospital (clerk)	T-52-A
	*Family * wife: Suzuko; first son: Takuya; first daughter: Mihoko; second daughter: Chisae			
(U)				
UCHIDA, Hiroshi (54)	Odaharu-mura, Chichibu-gun, Saitama Pref.	Brawley, California	Agriculture	EQ-94-4
	*Family * wife: Kumi; second son: Tenchi			

(*continued*)

CRYSTAL CITY REGISTRY JAPANESE FAMILY LIST February 11 1945 *(continued)*

Name (Age)	Primary Address	Previous Address	Occupation	Section No.
UCHIYAMA, Soichi (42)	Shiramizu-mura, Kamimasuki-gun, Kumamoto Pref.	Chiclayo, Peru, South America	Photography	D-52-A
	*Family * wife: Shizue; first son: Mutsuhiro; first daughter: Atsuko; second daughter: Maeko; third daughter: Masami; brother: Tomoichi			
UDO, Kazuji (60)	Yoneda-mura, Shikamoto-gun, Kumamoto Pref.	Hawthorne, California	Gardener	EQ-33-1
	*Family * wife: Toki; first son: Haruo; second son: Toshio; third daughter: Michiko			
UEHARA, Yoshinobu (35)	Ozato-mura, Shimajiri-gun, Okinawa Pref.	Lima, Peru, South America	Material shop	Q-64-3
	*Family * wife: Tsuruko			
UEHARA, Zensuke (45)	Hanechi-mura, Kokuto-gun, Okinawa Pref.	Lima, Peru, South America	Restanrant	Q-64-3
	*Family * wife: Toku; second son: Akira; third son: Yoshiaki; fourth son: Hideyoshi; third daughter: Toshiko; fourth daughter: Yasuko; fifth daughter: Yoko			
UMEKI, Masasuke (52)	Kajiki-cho, Shira-gun, Kagoshima Pref.	San Bernadino, California	Flower Gardener	Q-43-4
	*Family * wife: Tokue; first daughter: Fumi			

UNO, Kumemaro (58)	Kamakago-cho, Koishikawa-ku, Tokyo	Los Angeles, California	Vermin extermination	Q-46-3
	*Family * wife: Rikiko; fifth son: Akimaro; sixth son: Tomimaro; fourth daughter: Keiko			
UOZAKI, Shozo (46)	Kawanoishi-cho, Nishiuwa-gun, Ehime Pref.	Lima, Peru, South America	Material shop	V-19,20
	*Family * wife: Tsuruko; first son: Kaoru; second son: Toshiyuki; first daughter: Tomiko; second daughter: Utako; third daughter: Yaeko			
URA, Isataro (60)	Yamato-mura, Yamakado-gun, Fukuoka Pref.	Wararu, Peru, South America	Farming business	EQ-94-1
	*Family * wife: Sunako; second son: Toshiyuki; eighth daughter: Mieko; ninth daughter: Emiko; tenth daughter: Asako			
URA, Hosei (40)	Yamato-mura, Yamakado-gun, Fukuoka Pref.	Wararu, Peru, South America	Wholesaler	V-40
	*Family * wife: Sanami; first son: Wataru; first daughter: Yoshiko			
UTSUMI, Kaji (34)	Makioka-mura, Nakakawachi-gun, Osaka-fu	Wankaiyo, Peru, South America	N/A	Q-67-4
	*Family * first daughter: Masako			
UTSURIKAWA, Tokiji (67)	Sendai-city, Miyagi-Pref.	Los Angeles, Calfornia	Photo studio	T-37-B
	*Family * wife: Nobu; first daughter: Kiyoko			

(*continued*)

CRYSTAL CITY REGISTRY JAPANESE FAMILY LIST February 11 1945 *(continued)*

Name (Age)	Primary Address	Previous Address	Occupation	Section No.
UEHARA, Naohide (56)	Koriyama-mura, Hioki-gun, Kagoshima Pref.	Oakland, California	Shoe maker	T-38-A
	*Family * wife: Rei; first son: Tetsuro; first daughter: Emi			
UECHI, Hisataro (65)	Shimosato-cho, Higashimui-gun, Wakayama Pref.	San Diego, California	Sea products seller	D-56-A
	*Family * wife: Kirie; first son: Kikuo; second son: Saburo; first daughter: Hisae			
UESHIMA, Yasutake (51)	Chosei-mura, Kitamurayama-gun, Yamagata Pref.	Los Angeles, California	Missionary	D-54-A
	*Family * wife: You; first son: Yasukazu; first daughter: Reiko; second daughter: Kyoko			
(W)				
WADA, Mikio (40)	Nodani-mura, Mitsu-gun, Okayama Pref.	Los Angeles, California	N/A	Q-42-1
	*Family * wife: Kikue			
WADA, Otokichi (65)	Minamiashie-cho, Ashiegami-gun, Kanagawa Pref.	San Francisco, California	Cook	T-6-A
	*Family * wfe: Saku; second son: Yoshio; fourth daughter: Kiyono			

WADA, Umeo (41)	Umebayashi-mura, Tamana-gun, Kumamoto Pref.	Honolulu, Hawaii	Missionary	Q-45-2
	*Family * wife: Matsu; first daughter: Kaoru; second daughter: Kiyoko; third daughter: Sachiko			
WAKAYAMA, Shoichi (44)	Sanjo-cho, Hiroshima-city, Hiroshima Pref.	Sebastopol, California	Agriculture	D-36-A
	*Family * wife: Tomie; first son: Masaru; second son: Haruo; first daughter: Ayako; second daughter: Mariko			
WATANABE, Harukichi (43)	Shimakawa-mura, Nobuo-gun, Fukushima Pref.	Tarma, Peru, South America	Haberdashery	DV-110
	*Family * wife: Shiki; first son: Toshio; second son: Hiroshi; third son: Yoshio; first daughter: Haruko			
WATABE, Masahisa (59)	Tsukigata-mura, Azumi-gun, Fukusihma Pref.	Lima, Peru, South America	Restaurant	V-75
	*Family * wife: Shima; third daughter: Kimiko			
WATANABE, Rikiei (49)	Harano-mura, Aima-gun, Fukushiama Pref.	Lima, Peru, South America	Material shop	V-74
	*Family * wife: Ishi; third daughter: Maruha			

(*continued*)

CRYSTAL CITY REGISTRY JAPANESE FAMILY LIST February 11 1945 *(continued)*

Name (Age)	Primary Address	Previous Address	Occupation	Section No.
WATANABE, Sanzo (53)	Kanetanigawa-mura, Nobuo-gun, Fukushima Pref.	Wararu, Peru, South America	Agriculture	V-54
	*Family * wife: Shina; first daughter: Kiyoko; second daughter: Asako; third daughter: Hanako			
WATANABE, Kozo (56)	Matsuura-mura, Kitakamohara-gun, Niigata Pref.	Seattle, Washington	Cleaning	T-39-C
	*Family * wife: Hiro			
(Y)				
YAGI, Shigeru (40)	Yoshikawa-mura, Yoshishiki-gun, Yamaguchi Pref.	Redondo Beach, California	Agriculture	T-29-B
	*Family * OTANI, Fusayo, OTANI, Satoru			
YAKABI, Seiji (52)	Ginowan-mura, Chuto-gun, Okinawa Pref.	Wacho, Peru, South America	Bakery	EQ-92-3
	*Family * wife: Makato; grand daughter: Naeko			
YAGI, Norisada (59)	Sakiyama-cho, Kubisato-city, Okinawa Pref.	Lima, Peru, South America	Office clerk	V-69
	*Family * wife: Mochi; first son: Hiruma; second daughter: Noriko			

YAMA, Manabu (46)	Yatomi-mura, Tamana-gun, Kumamoto Pref.	Honolulu, Hawaii	Priest of Tenri-kyo	Q-41-2
	*Family * wife: Kazue; first son: Toshihiro; second son: Hironori; third son: Toshio; first daughter: Kikuko			
YAMAGISHI, Seiji (46)	Tsushima-cho, Kaibe-gun, Aichi Pref.	Stockton, California	Cleaning	D-60-B
	*Family * wife: Hatsue; first son: Kiyoshi; second son: Noboru; third son: Mitsuru			
YAMAGUCHI, Genji (42)	Minamisaigo-mura, Sampo-gun, Fukui Pref.	Los Angeles, California	Agriculture	Q-45-4
	*Family * wife: Chieko; first son: Takeshi; second son: Makoto; third son: Michihiro; first daughter: Sumie			
YAMAKAWA, Yoshinobu (41)	Iwakiji-mura, Kokuto-gun, Okinawa Pref	Hilo, Hawaii	Teacher	Q-47-2
	*Family * wife: Fujiko			
YAMAMOTO, Eiichi (47)	Kami-mura, Numakuma-gun, Hiroshima Pref.	Petaluma, California	Poultry farming	D-36-B
	*Family * wife: Hisano; first son: Yukio; second son: Hiroshi; first daughter: Eiko			

(*continued*)

CRYSTAL CITY REGISTRY JAPANESE FAMILY LIST February 11 1945 *(continued)*

Name (Age)	Primary Address	Previous Address	Occupation	Section No.
YAMAMOTO, Hanpei (52)	Nakayama-mura, Shimomasuki-gun, Kumamoto Pref.	Visco, Peru, South America	Material shop	V-56
	*Family * wife: Matsue; second daughter: Sumie; third daughter: Harue; fourth daughter: Natsumi			
YAMAMOTO, Kanesaku (48)	Itsukaichi-cho, Saeki-gun, Hiroshima Pref.	Chiclayo, Peru, South America	Business	Q-64-4
	*Family * wife: Hatsuyo			
YAMAMOTO, Koichi (48)	Isa-mura, Miya-gun, Yamaguchi Pref	Berkeley, California	Cleaning	DV-128-A
	*Family * wife: Yamato; first daughter: Kiyoko; second daughter: Kikuko; third daughter: Sumiko; fourth daughter: Aiko; fifth daughter: Etsuko			
YAMAMOTO, Mitsuyoshi (39)	Shinan-mura, Takata-gun, Shizuoka Pref.	Pescadero, California	Agriculture	D-50-B
	*Family * wife: Mitsue; first son: Kenichi; second son: Takashi; first daughter: Aiko; second daughter: Mieko			
YAMAMOTO, Ototaro (42)	Saijo-cho, Kure-city, Hiroshima Pref.	San Gabriel, California	Gardener	D-14-A
	*Family * wife: Matsue; first son: Michitaro; second son: Kikujiro; third son: Teruo; fourth son: Takeo; first daughter: Asako			

YAMAMOTO, Yoshitomo (32)	Sano, Shingu-city, Wakayama Pref.	Lima, Peru, South America	Office clerk	EQ-72-4
	*Family * wife: Tamiko; first son: Kazunori			
YAMANE, Saburo (44)	Kariogawa-mura, Asa-gun, Hiroshima Pref.	Los Angeles, California	Business	D-41-A
	*Family * wife: Sadako; first son: Hiroshi; first daughter: Teruko; second daughter: Akiko; third daughter: Nobuko; fourth daughter: Kumiko			
YAMANE, Seiichi (58)	Iwakuni-city, Yamaguchi Pref.	Honolulu, Hawaii	House rental	T-34-B
	*Family * wife: Tsuta			
YAMASAKI, Jokichi (45)	Nishikimi, Iwakuni-city, Yamaguchi Pref	Wacho, Peru, South America	Blacksmith	Q-69-1
	*Family * wife: Tamako			
YAMASAKI, Sotoji (31)	Keya-cho, Fukui-city, Fukui Pref.	Wacho, Peru, South America	Business	Q-68-4
	*Family * wife: Masue; first son: Hiroaki			
YAMASAKI, Tadashi (38)	Keya-cho, Fukui-city, Fukui Pref.	Wacho, Peru, South America	Business	D-24-B
	*Family * wife: Setsuko; first son: Toshihiko; second son: Masaki; third son: Akira; first daughter: Kayoko; second daughter: Naomi; third daughter: Hidemi			

(*continued*)

CRYSTAL CITY REGISTRY JAPANESE FAMILY LIST February 11 1945 *(continued)*

Name (Age)	Primary Address	Previous Address	Occupation	Section No.
YAMAZATO, Toshio (44)	Hanechi-mura, Kokuto-gun, Okinawa Pref.	Lima, Peru, South America	Haberdashery	V-35
	*Family * wife: Yasu; first son: Hiroyasu; first daughter: Hisako; second daughter: Sachiko			
YAMASHIRO, Yukinori (43)	Hanechi-mura, Kokuto-gun, Okinawa Pref.	Liberta, Peru, South America	Business	V-1,2
	*Family * first son: Hiroshi; second son: Isamu; third son: August; fourth son: Daniel; fifth son: Edward; sixth son: Hilmen; seventh son: Adolph			
YAMASHITA, Akimitsu (34)	Nagara-mura, Gifu-city, Gifu Pref.	Los Angeles, California	Missionary	D-37-A
	*Family * wife: Shizue; first son: Tetsumune; first daughter: Reiko; second daughter: Hiromi			
YASUDA, Masato (41)	Fuchu-cho, Hiroshima-city, Hiroshima Pref.	Los Angeles, California	Business	D-41-B
	*Family * wife: Kiyoko;first son: Yoshio; second son: Noboru; first daughter: Masako			
YASUDA, Seiichi (40)	Kaminoseki-mura, Kumage-gun, Yamaguchi Pref.	Mesa, Arizona	Business	T-33-A
	*Family * wife: Tsuruko; third son: Eisaburo; fourth son: Seishiro; second daughter: Fumiko			

YATOMI, Aiko (23)	Sanyo-mura, Ukiha-gun, Fukuoka Pref.	Lima, Peru, South America	N/A	Q-47-1
	*Family * first son: Akio; first daughter: Yuriko			
YODA, Masao (39)	Minobe-cho, Minamishima-gun, Yamanashi Pref.	Lima, Peru, South America	Business	Q-47-4
	*Family * wife: Masuko			
YOGI, Hironori (30)	Honbu-cho, Kokuto-gun, Okinawa Pref.	Lima, Peru, South America	Haberdashery	T-12-A
	*Family * wife: Toshi, first son: Hirosada; first daughter: Hiroko			
YOGI, Yoshiki (38)	Ozato-mura, Shimajiri-gun, Okinawa Pref.	Lima, Peru, South America	Teacher	D-58-A
	*Family * wife: Kikuko; first son: Ken; second son: Tamotsu; third son: Susumu			
YOGI, Shigeo (41)	Nakajo-mura, Chuto-gun, Okinawa Pref.	Lima, Peru, South America	Teacher	T-11-BC
	*Family * wife: Uto; first son: Tetsuya; first daughter: Setsuko; second daughter: Akiko; third daughter: Misako			
YONEKURA, Hashiyoshi (53)	Kuroda-mrua, Kawaki-gun, Mie Pref.	Chula Vista, California	Agriculture	D-56-B
	*Family * wife: Riu; first son: Masakatsu; second son: Akira; third son: Toshiharu			

(*continued*)

CRYSTAL CITY REGISTRY JAPANESE FAMILY LIST February 11 1945 *(continued)*

Name (Age)	Primary Address	Previous Address	Occupation	Section No.
YOSHIDA, Itsuji (37)	Yunoe-cho, Kitatakaki-gun, Nagasaki Pref.	Chiclayo, Peru, South America	Business	T-43-B
	*Family * wife: Ai; first daughter: Teruyo			
YOSHIDA, Masao (33)	Yunoe-cho, Kitatakaki-gun, Nagasaki Pref.	Chiclayo, Peru, South America	Business	Q-63-4
	*Family * wife: Kikue; first daughter: Tomoko; second daughter: Keiko			
YOSHIDA, Kunita (40)	Wada-mura, Oshima-gun, Yamaguchi Pref	Kaniete, Peru, South America	Material shop	V-67
	*Family * wife: Tomiyo; first son: Akio; first daughter: Yasuko; second daughter: Katsuko			
YOSHIDA, Susumu (35)	Kawarakouji, Saga-city, Saga Pref.	Los Angeles, California	Priest of Tenri-kyo	D-58-B
	*Family * wife: Shigeko; first son: Hajime; second son: Toshiro; first daughter: Ikuko; second daughter: Minoru			
YOSHIMURA, Kensaku (45)	Itsukaichi-cho, Saeki-gun, Hiroshima Pref.	Delano, California	Agriculture	D-42-B
	*Family * wife: Chieko; first son: Shigeru			

YOSHIMURA, Susumu (43)	Yasuhara-mura, Umikusa-gun, Wakayama Pref.	Suisun, California	Agriculture	T-61-A
	*Family * wife: Yoshiko; first son: Haruo; first daughter: Uzuki			
YOSHINAGA, Kahei (57)	Sotoikenoue, Kumamoto-city, Kumamoto Pref.	Ica, Peru, South America	Business	V-10
	*Family * wife: Tsumo; third daughter: Fumiko			
YOSHIOKA, Tokuichi (58)	Chiomae-mura, Saeki-gun, Hiroshima Pref.	Lima, Peru, South America	Blacksmith	EQ-72-3
	*Family * wife: Kaneko; first daughter: Satoko; second daughter: Mitsuko; third daughter: Mieko			
YOSHIZAWA, Seizo (75)	Iida-city, Shimoina-gun, Nagano Pref.	Petaluma, California	Poultry farming	T-62-B
	*Family * wife: Yuki			
YUKI, Wakijiro (59)	Tajima-mura, Munakata-gun, Fukuoka Pref.	Los Gatos, California	Agriculture	Q-39-1
	*Family * wife: Kimino; third son: Masato; third daughter: Chiyoka			
YUTANI, Goroichi (63)	Odera-cho, Higashimui-gun, Wakayama Pref.	Terminal Island, California	Fishery	Q-45-1
	*Family * wife: Fumiyo			

(*continued*)

CRYSTAL CITY REGISTRY JAPANESE FAMILY LIST February 11 1945 *(continued)*

Name (Age)	Primary Address	Previous Address	Occupation	Section No.
(Z)				
ZUIKO, Shigematsu (57)	Irino-mura, Toyoda-gun, Hiroshima Pref.	Wacho, Peru, South America	Agriculture	EQ-78-3
	*Family * wife: Kama; second son: Shigetaka; third son: Shigefusa; fourth son: Mineto; first daughter: Sadae; second daughter: Fusae; third daughter: Miyoko			
(Additional)				
ITAHARA, Kumashige (55)	Takaoka-cho, Takaoka-gun, Kochi Pref.	Santa Ana, California	Agriculture	DV-133-A
	*Family * wife: Kikuyo			
ITO, Ryusaburo (60)	Wakayagi-cho, Kurihara-gun, Miyagi Pref	Oakland, California	Insurance company	DV-152-A
	*Family * wife: Kane; first son: Shigeru; first daughter: Kiyoko; third daughter: Yoneko			
KAWANAMI, Sota (64)	Aida-mura, Mitsui-gun, Fukuoka Pref	Calexico, California	Farming products transportation	DV-130-B
	*Family * wife: Tomo; first son: Kenichi; second son: Masao; third son: Hideo; second daughter: Kiyoko			

MORITA, Takuritsu (57)	Taiseiji-cho, Enuma-gun, Ishikawa Pref.	Mountain View, California	Teacher	DV-148, 151B
	*Family * wife: Toyo; second son: Jiro; third son: Mitsuo; fourth son: Shiro; fifth son: Itsuo; first daughter: Takako; second daughter: Tetsuko; third daughter: Setsuko			
MORITA, Toichiro (61)	Yasuno-mura, Yamagata-gun, Hiroshima Pref.	Riverside, California	Agriculture	DV-132-B
	*Family * wife: Tatsu; second daughter: Akemi; third daughter: Emi			
MOTOIKE, Fusaichi (63)	Uemichi-mura, Nishieki-gun, Tottori Pref.	Redondo Beach, California	Agriculture	DV-135-A
	*Family * wife: Kae			
NAKANO, Taoto (58)	Obata-mura, Kamiishi-gun, Hiroshima Pref.	San Diego, Calfornia	Agriculture	DV-144-A
	*Family * wife: Kotono; second son: Hiroshi; third son: Shigeru; fifth son: Tsutomu; sixth son: Akira; seventh son: Isamu; second daughter: Masako			
NISHI, Kiyotaro (60)	Kushimoto-cho, Nishimui-gun, Wakayama Pref	San Francisco, California	Office clerk	DV-145-B
	*Family * wife: Fukino; adopted son: AKAGAKI, Masao			

(*continued*)

CRYSTAL CITY REGISTRY JAPANESE FAMILY LIST February 11 1945 *(continued)*

Name (Age)	Primary Address	Previous Address	Occupation	Section No.
SERA, Kyoichi (48)	Miyauchi-mura, Saeki-gun, Hiroshima Pref.	Visalia, California	Agriculture	DV-103
	*Family * wife: Toku; first son: Masamitsu; third son: Hiroshi; fourth son: Yutaka; fifth son: Kaoru; sixth son: Katsuo; first daughter: Tamae			
TANITA, Masato (55)	Fukagawa-mura, Asa-gun, Hiroshima Pref.	Vista, California	Agriculture	DV-136-AB
	*Family * wife: Sumi; first son: Hoshio; second son: Yuzuru; third son: Shozo; first daughter: Fumiko; second daughter: Yoshie; third daughter: Tadako; fourth daughter: Katsuko			
TSUYUKI, Taichi (32)	Shinan-mura, Takata-gun, Shizuoka Pref.	Los Angeles, California	Priest of Tenri-kyo	DV-127-B
	*Family * wife: Yoshie; first son: Masahisa; second son: Akiyoshi			
RIHASHI, Kosaku (46)	Tomigata-mura, Kamiina-gun, Nagano Pref.	Los Angeles, California	Gardener	DV-134-A
	*Family * wife: Shizuko; first daughter: Tomoko			
WATANABE, Tatsuo (56)	Chide-mura, Kaho-gun, Fukuoka Pref.	Vista, California	Gardener	DV-132-A
	*Family * wife: Sumi			

Appendix 4

All photos courtesy of Joy Tsuzuki.

Hideo's American born niece Sochiko, nephew Richard, and daughter Joy at the Ashbury Park Broadwalk, New Jersey, in the 1930's.

Joy, Fusako, and Hideo at a park across the street from their home in New York City, in 1938.

Joy, Fusako, and Hideo in New York City, in 1938.

Hideo and Fusako in their home with several injured US Occupation Army Officers.

Hideo, Fusako, and Joy at home in Meguro, Tokyo, in 1948.

Toshio, Joy, Hideo, and Fusako in Tokyo, 1950.

Hideo and Fusako at home in Meguro, Tokyo, 1950.

Hideo in his office, in 1950.

Appendix 5

Joint Army and Navy Basic War Plan Orange—1924 Version

SECRET

SECRETARY
ROOM 2743
NAVY DEPARTMENT BUILDING

THE JOINT BOARD
JOINT PLANNING COMMITTEE
WASHINGTON

From: The Joint Planning Committee.

To: The Joint Board.

Subject: Joint Army and Navy Basic War Plan - Orange.

Reference: (a) J. B. No. 207 of 7 July, 1923. Synopsis of Joint Army and Navy Estimates of the Orange Situation.

(b) J. B. No. 208 of 7 July, 1923. Defense of Philippines.

Inclosure: (A) Joint Army and Navy Basic War Plan - Orange.

1. Reference (a) directs that The Joint Board submit a Joint Basic Plan to make the decisions stated in reference (a) effective.

2. In accordance therewith the Joint Planning Committee submits herewith Joint Army and Navy Basic War Plan - Orange (Inclosure A).

WM. H. STANDLEY,
Captain, U. S. Navy.

J. L. DeWITT,
Colonel, General Staff.

SECRET

THE JOINT BOARD
JOINT PLANNING COMMITTEE
WASHINGTON

JOINT ARMY AND NAVY BASIC WAR PLAN - ORANGE

I. GENERAL CONCLUSIONS OF THE JOINT ARMY AND NAVY ESTIMATE OF THE SITUATION.

1. Any great war in the Pacific involving the United States will, so far as can be foreseen, be with Japan.

2. In the event of such a war, the war aims of the United States, stated in general terms, will be -

To force Japan to a settlement satisfactory to the United States, of the issues that caused the war.

3. In order to attain its war aims, the United States, if Japan has no European allies, will have to achieve success in the Western Pacific.

4. The first and governing concern of the Army and Navy in such a war will accordingly be:

To establish, at the earliest date, American sea power in the Western Pacific in strength superior to that of Japan.

5. Such action will depend upon founding a main outlying base in the Western Pacific, capable of serving the entire U. S. Fleet.

6. Manila Bay is our strongest point in the Western Pacific and is the best available site in that region for such a main outlying base.

7. War in the Western Pacific will require docking and repair facilities in that region for all classes of vessels, and secure lines of communication from the United States.

8. American success in the Western Pacific will probably require:

(a) The holding or retaking of Manila Bay.

(b) The occupation or control of all harbors in the islands mandated to Japan and in the Philippines.

(c) The effective control of the vital sea communications of Japan.

(d) Offensive sea and air operations against Japanese naval forces and economic life.

(e) Such further action as will compel Japanese submission.

II. DECISION.

GENERAL CONCEPT OF THE WAR.

AN OFFENSIVE WAR, PRIMARILY NAVAL, DIRECTED TOWARD THE ISOLATION AND HARASSMENT OF JAPAN, THROUGH CONTROL OF HER VITAL SEA COMMUNICATIONS AND THROUGH OFFENSIVE SEA AND AIR OPERATIONS AGAINST HER NAVAL FORCES AND ECONOMIC LIFE, COUPLED WITH SUCH FURTHER ACTION AS WILL COMPEL JAPANESE SUBMISSION.

III. PHASES OF THE WAR.

1. The following steps are necessary to make effective the General Concept of the War:

(a) To establish, at the earliest date, American sea power in the Western Pacific in strength superior to that of Japan; and

(b) To take such further action as will make effective the General Concept of the War.

2. The foregoing steps naturally divide the war into the corresponding phases:

(a) The Initial Phase, during which the interests of the Navy are paramount; beginning on D (zero) day and ending when American sea power has been established in the Western Pacific in strength superior to that of Japan; and

(b) The Subsequent Phase, during which the interests of the Army or of the Navy may be paramount; beginning upon completion of the Initial Phase and ending with the termination of hostilities.

IV. JOINT GENERAL MISSION OF THE ARMY AND NAVY.

TO MAKE EFFECTIVE THE GENERAL CONCEPT OF THE WAR.

This involves:

1. Joint Initial Mission of the Army and Navy.

TO ESTABLISH AT THE EARLIEST DATE, AMERICAN SEA POWER IN THE WESTERN PACIFIC IN STRENGTH SUPERIOR TO THAT OF JAPAN.

The Initial Mission involves the following Contributory Missions:

(a) To hold Manila Bay.

(b) To make ready for –

(1) An immediate naval advance with land reinforcements for Manila.

(2) Subsequent Naval and Army reinforcements and replacements in sufficient force to make effective the general concept of the war.

(3) A long war, primarily maritime.

(4) The early capture, occupation, or control of all anchorages in the islands mandated to Japan and in the Philippines.

(5) The development and use of Army and Navy air power overwhelmingly.

(c) To operate with boldness from the earliest stages of the war and to seek the initiative in all operations.

(d) To encourage preparations, within American industry and other branches of the government, that will mobilize American resources toward:

(1) Developing at the earliest date adequate logistic support, first for the Navy, second for the Army.

(2) Building at once movable floating docks for the Navy.

(3) Providing adequate fuel supply for the Navy.

(4) Developing to the maximum American ship-building.

2. Joint Subsequent Mission of the Army and Navy.

To take such further action as will make effective the general concept of the war.

V. GENERAL MISSION OF THE NAVY.

Jointly with the Army, to make effective the general concept of the war. This involves:

1. Initial Mission of the Navy.

Jointly with the Army, to establish, at the earliest date, American sea power in the Western Pacific in strength superior to that of Japan.

This should include as initial steps:

(a) Such a prevision and such a strategic disposition and degree of readiness, in peace time, of the United States Fleet and Naval Transportation Service as will permit the concentration at the Hawaiian Islands by D (zero) plus ten days of a force of active units at least 50% superior to the total Japanese naval strength, and as will permit commencement of the movement to Manila Bay of this force and the Army reinforcements (see paragraph 1 (a), Section VI), by D (zero) plus fourteen days.

(b) Readiness of the entire Naval Establishment to support and sustain this concentration and movement.

(c) Provision for adequate mobile base facilities, particularly floating drydocks and fuel supply.

(d) Provision for procuring, manning, and operating by the Navy of all vessels employed at sea for the Army Transportation Service, all ports of embarkation therefor to be established, operated, and maintained by the Army.

2. Subsequent Mission of the Navy.

Jointly with the Army, to take such further action as will make effective the general concept of the war.

VI. GENERAL MISSION OF THE ARMY.

Jointly with the Navy, to make effective the general concept of the war. This involves:

1. Initial Mission of the Army.

Jointly with the Navy, to establish, at the earliest date, American sea power in the Western Pacific in strength superior to that of Japan.

This should include as initial steps:

(a) Making available at loading ports on the Pacific Coast of the United States for transportation by the Navy to Oahu, one Army Corps of at least 50,000 troops in time to arrive in Oahu by D (zero) plus ten days. This force will be ready to leave the Hawaiian Islands by D (zero) plus fourteen days, it being understood that the promptest possible reinforcement of Manila Bay is of the greatest military and naval importance. Essential organizational equipment for this force will be stored in the Philippines in time of peace, in order to reduce war time transportation required to the minimum.

(b) Making available by D (zero) plus thirty days at loading ports on the Pacific Coast of the United States an additional force of troops for transportation by the Navy to the points indicated below for the purpose of -

(1) Relieving the Fleet Expeditionary Force of Marines in the Marshall and Caroline Islands and garrisoning those islands.

(2) Recapturing Guam.

(c) Making available by D (zero) plus thirty days at loading ports on the Pacific and Atlantic Coasts of the United States for transportation by the Navy to Oahu and the Panama Canal, respectively, of the troops required for raising the garrisons of those places to the war strength specified in their respective Defense Projects.

(d) Mobilizing and holding in reserve in Continental United States such troops, in addition to the foregoing, as are considered necessary to meet unforeseen contingencies.

(e) Establishing, operating and maintaining all ports of embarkation for the Army Transportation Service, all vessels employed at sea for that service to be procured, manned and operated by the Navy.

2. Subsequent Mission of the Army.

Jointly with the Navy, to take such further action as will make effective the general concept of the war.

VII. CONDUCT OF JOINT OPERATIONS CONTEMPLATED IN THIS PLAN.

1. General Principles.

The magnitude of the joint operations contemplated in the principal theater of operations and the difficulties likely to be encountered in carrying them to a successful conclusion at a great distance from home require:

(a) That all Army and Navy forces within the principal theater of operations form a single command.

(b) That the whole responsibility and full power commensurate therewith for carrying out the operations contemplated in this plan and for initiating and controlling all operations growing out of it, within the principal theater of operations, be confided to a single commander.

(c) That this commander be assisted by a Joint Army and Navy Staff.

(d) That the efforts of the War and Navy Departments, in so far as planning for and initiation and execution of preparatory measures for the contemplated operations are concerned, be coordinated by the Joint Board.

2. Command.

(a) All Army and Navy forces within the principal theater of operations, including at the discretion of the Commander-in-Chief, U.S.A.E.F., the Army forces in Alaska, shall form one command and shall be designated as "United States Asiatic Expeditionary Forces," abbreviated "U.S.A.E.F."

(b) The U. S.A.E.F. shall be under command of an officer designated as "Commander-in-Chief, United States Asiatic Expeditionary Forces", who shall have the whole responsibility and full power commensurate therewith for carrying out the operations contemplated in this plan and for initiating and controlling all operations growing out of it within the principal theater of operations.

(c) The Commander-in-Chief, U.S.A.E.F., shall be assisted by a Joint Army and Navy Staff, composed of a suitable number of Army and Navy officers detailed by the Secretary of War and the Secretary of the Navy upon the recommendation of the Commander-in-Chief, U.S.A.E.F.

(d) The Headquarters of the Commander-in-Chief, U.S.A.E.F., shall be designated as "G.H.Q., U.S.A.E.F."

(e) During the Initial Phase of the war - indicated in Section III, paragraph 2 (a) hereof - the Commander-in-Chief, U. S. Fleet, shall be the Commander-in-Chief, U.S.A.E.F.

(f) During the Subsequent Phase of the war - indicated in Section III, paragraph 2 (b) hereof - an officer to be designated by the President, prior to the termination of the Initial Phase, shall be the Commander-in-Chief, U.S.A.E.F., the passage of command, in the event that a new officer is designated as Commander-in-Chief, being arranged by mutual agreement between the Commanders concerned.

VIII. <u>THEATERS OF OPERATIONS.</u>

1. <u>Principal Theater of Operations.</u>

The area west of one hundred and forty (140) degrees west longitude, and east of one hundred (100) degrees east longitude, exclusive of Alaska, which may, however, be included at the discretion of the Commander-in-Chief, U.S.A.E.F.

2. Secondary Theaters of Operations.

Such other theaters of operations as may be designated if and when occasion therefor arises.

IX. ARMY AND NAVY PLANS.

1. The foregoing Joint Army and Navy Basic War Plan - Orange, when approved by the Secretary of War and the Secretary of the Navy, will constitute the basis upon which the Army War Plan - Orange and the Navy War Plan - Orange will be formulated and developed.

2. When any question of jurisdiction and responsibility arises that requires interpretation of this basic plan, the matter will be referred to the Joint Board for decision.